Ridgecrest
Mountain of Faith

Kenneth McAnear

©Copyright 1982
Reprinted 1997
All Rights reserved

4265-66
ISBN 0-8054-6566-9

Dewey Decimal Classification: 28606
Subject Heading: RIDGECREST BAPTIST CONFERENCE CENTER
Library of Congress Catalog Card Number: 81-67325

Printed in the United States of America

All Scripture quotations are from the
King James Version of the Bible.

The Sunday School Board of
the Southern Baptist Convention
127 Ninth Avenue North
Nashville, TN 37234

Dedication

*To Ann
my beloved wife, fellow servant
in the ministry of Christ,
and mother of our children,
Paul, Kendra, and Martha*

Foreword

God used B. W. Spilman's vision and efforts to establish Ridgecrest Baptist Conference Center. Spilman was driven by his desire to provide a place where Southern Baptists could gather in the summer to learn how to be effective Sunday School workers. As they learned, they worshiped, made spiritual decisions that impacted their lives for eternity, and forged memories that would last a lifetime.

Because of Ridgecrest's contribution to churches and to persons' lives, the Southern Baptist Convention saw the need for a second assembly in the West. The new center was located at Glorieta, New Mexico, and the first conference was held there in 1952.

At Ridgecrest and Glorieta, legions have heard and responded to God's call. Thousands of pastors, missionaries, and church staff persons can point to a moment at Ridgecrest or Glorieta when they committed their lives to Christ or vocational ministry. Multitudes of laypersons have gained skills for church and campus ministries.

For example, David Blanton, minister of youth at Terry Parker Baptist Church in Jacksonville, Florida, said Ridgecrest had enabled him to "have a personal encounter with God on the 'mountain of faith,' meet friends across the years, be part of God's plan to bring young people to Ridgecrest, see them saved or recommit their lives to God, see God call young people into ministry, and have the opportunity of rejoicing with them as well as have my own faith recharged and the sense of my call into His service renewed."

When Jerry Davis, president of the College of the Ozarks in Point Lookout, Missouri, first visited Ridgecrest, he was a troubled teenager from a dysfunctional family. Davis recalled, "I needed an identity, a supportive family, close friends, a life partner, and a purpose for life. God gave me all this through Ridgecrest. I can never repay that debt. To this day Ridgecrest casts rays of light across my life and the life of my family. We have accumulated over 50 summers of life-changing experiences while attending or working on staff at the conference center and Camp Ridgecrest."

Your life will be changed forever as you meet God at Ridgecrest, seek His will for your life, and gain new skills for Christian service.

James T. Draper, Jr.
April 1997

Preface

The 75th anniversary of Ridgecrest Baptist Conference Center will be commemorated throughout 1982. An updated history of the conference center was requested as part of this celebration. Each summer we receive numerous requests from those attending conferences for a history of the conference center.

I gladly accepted the assignment to write this book. My personal appreciation for the conference center and its ministry to Southern Baptists made the writing enjoyable.

I gratefully acknowledge the contributions of many who through the years have written brief histories, collected documents for historical files, and in other ways made valuable memorabilia of Ridgecrest's history available. I have referenced these sources in the text and have footnoted them when appropriate and data was available. Many other contributions are not identified but are gratefully acknowledged.

History is people, buildings and assets, and visible accomplishments. More than anything else, Christian history is God working through persons to accomplish His will in the lives of His people and to call all people to Himself. The purpose of this book is to show God's active role in the development and growth of Ridgecrest. I offer this book to His glory.

My thanks go to Karen Lomaz and Electra Campbell for their valuable assistance in typing the manuscript. Special thanks go to my wife, Ann, who read and evaluated the manuscript.

Ken McAnear
Ridgecrest, North Carolina
1982

Contents

1. The Making of a Mountain 7
2. A Man for the Mountain 11
3. Claiming the Mountain 15
4. Financing the Mountain 19
5. Testing Their Faith 23
6. Programming by Faith 31
7. The Education Board Years 37
8. Years of Transition 53
9. Faith Vindicated 61
10. Beyond the Dream 67
11. A Developing Mountain 73
12. Tomorrow: A New Day of Faith 83

    Appendix 1: Tributes 87
        James H. Tucker
        B. W. Spilman
        Willard K. Weeks

    Appendix 2: Camp Ridgecrest for Boys and
        Camp Crestridge for Girls 91

    Appendix 3: Ridgecrest Employees: People of Faith 99

    Appendix 4: Glorieta Baptist Conference Center 101

    Postscript 103

1 The Making of a Mountain

In the beginning God. . . (Gen. 1:1).

The Swannanoa Valley nestles in the foothills of the majestic Appalachian Mountains. This serene valley seems to have been prepared by the Creator to become the home of Ridgecrest Baptist Conference Center.

Swannanoa Valley is surrounded by a 35-mile range of mountains, including the Blue Ridge and Black Mountains. Mount Mitchell, the highest point in North American east of the Rocky Mountains, towers in full view of the valley. Other heralded peaks that rise above the surrounding mountain range are Great Craggy Dome and Clingman Dome. With only one narrow outlet, and that located to the west, the Ridgecrest area remained virtually inaccessible for years after the neighboring region was settled.

The mountains protected the valley and served as a valuable watershed for the acres of comparatively level land on the valley floor. Through the years, these mountain streams have supplied water to residents and God's woodland creatures. Today these streams remain the main water source for the valley and the city of Asheville, North Carolina, which is located at the western mouth of the Swannanoa Valley.

The climate includes four seasons of unsurpassed, delightful, health-giving beauty. Because of the pure air and icy, clear mountain streams, the first "industry" of the area was care of the sick. Today the area's climate and scenic beauty combine to make the valley known for its spiritual healing as well as for the mental and physical ministry of its earlier days.

Within a 35-mile radius of Ridgecrest Baptist Conference Center, more than 50 church-related conference centers, YMCA and private camps minister to well over 100 thousand people each year. Almost every major denomination is represented by one or more centers in the area.

Like many of the centers, Ridgecrest is located in the mountains surrounding the Swannanoa Valley. The Baptist conference center stands at the eastern gate of the valley near the Eastern Continental Divide. The streams that cross the Ridgecrest campus combine to become the headwaters of the Swannanoa River that flows west. Streams on the backside of the Divide flow east to form the Catawba River.

For years, the mountain where Ridgecrest now stands was considered inaccessible from the east. North Carolina's development stopped at the eastern foot of the mountains near Old Fort. For centuries the land lay untouched by the invasions of settlers. Pioneers arrived in the Swannanoa area less than 150 years before Ridgecrest was incorporated. It seemed as if God had saved the area until "the fullness of the time" and then swiftly opened the door and prepared the hearts of people to develop Ridgecrest Conference Center for His glory.

The area's early days did not reflect the Christian image of its later development. Typical of the frontier movement, the Ridgecrest region was opened with war. In August 1776, when the colonies were declaring their independence from England, troops entered the valley on the eastern side of the mountain to "rid" western North Carolina and eastern Tennessee of Cherokee residents.

General Griffith Rutherford, with 2,400 North Carolinians, left Davidson's Fort (later Old Fort) and scaled the mighty mountains that had stood for so long as a barrier to the Ridgecrest region's development and had separated North Carolina's lowlands on the east from the mountain highlands to the west. The winding, treacherous curves of U.S. 70 highway remind present-day travelers of the difficulties facing this army. The highway follows the same twisting, turning trail followed by Rutherford.

When Rutherford reached the area that is now Ridgecrest, the beauty of the valley must have spoken to him of God's special handiwork. He proclaimed the place "Eden Land." A variety of trees covered the mountains. Rhododendron, mountain laurel, dogwood, and sourwood all added their beauty to the scene. The splendor of August colors and the flowers in bloom would have caused anyone to pause in amazement at the beauty of "paradise rediscovered."

By 1780, settlers had followed Rutherford's steps and had built homes in the fertile Swannanoa Valley. In 1784, Colonel Samuel W. Davidson developed the first permanent settlement in the area. Further development was rapid, considering the times and the lack of accessibility to the area. By 1848, records show the existence of a school in Grey Eagle, known today as Black Mountain.

One of the world's great engineering and construction achievements, putting a railroad through this region, was nearing completion. Nine miles of railroad track climbed almost 1,100 feet while covering only three and four tenths miles by air.

On March 11, 1879, the "great opening" came as the railroad entered the Swannanoa Valley. Governor Zebulon Baird Vance received a telegram from James W. Wilson, president, superintendent, and chief engineer for the Western North Carolina Railroad. The telegram read: "Daylight entered Buncombe County today through Swannanoa Tunnel. Grade and centers met exactly." The telegram referred to the Swannanoa tunnel which travels underground for 1,828 feet at the mountain's crest. This was the longest of seven tunnels. The shortest was 89 feet.

With the building of the railroad, the valley was open east and west and the mountains were ready for people of vision and wisdom.

Mountains are a biblical symbol of God's presence, stability, and strength. Moses climbed a mountain to receive the law, to commune with God, and to learn of His wisdom. He also climbed a mountain to view the land God had given Israel. Jesus went to a mountain to pray. The disciples experienced the transfiguration on a mountain. Jesus' great sermon was delivered on a mountain. Through the ages men and women have scaled mountain peaks in search of the serenity that comes from God's presence.

Dr. Hight C. Moore called the dream of the Ridgecrest founders the "magnificent obsession." The founders envisioned the mountains as a place where, throughout the year, multitudes might meet Jesus and where, with Him and each other, "they might cherish and cultivate eternal friendships." Ridgecrest was to be a place where "wearied workers longing for the tonic of bracing air, inspiring summit, and distant view, might hearken to the Master's word, 'Come ye apart . . . and rest awhile.' "[1]

The men who founded Ridgecrest surely realized the educational values of the mountains that were reflected in the words of Dr. John A. Broadus when in 1874 he wrote of John the Baptist: "He was a child of the mountains. Whenever education and religion take hold in a mountain region, the result is great strength of character."[2]

The prophet Micah's words could be applied to Ridgecrest: "But in the last days it shall come to pass, that the mountain of the house of the LORD shall be established in the top of the mountains, and it shall be exalted above the hills; and the people shall flow unto it. And many nations shall come, and say, Come, and let us go to the mountain of the LORD, and to the house of the God of Jacob; and he will teach us of his ways, and we will walk in his paths" (Mic. 4:1–2a).

The mountain of faith was ready. Men of faith were being prepared. The birth of Ridgecrest Baptist Conference Center was near.

---

[1] Hight C. Moore, *The Story of Ridgecrest* (Nashville: Broadman Press, 1950), 5.
[2] Cited from the unpublished notes of John A. Broadus and quoted by A. T. Robertson in *John the Loyal* (Nashville: Broadman Press, 1977), 26.

2 A Man for the Mountain

I thank Christ Jesus our Lord, who hath enabled me, for that he counted me faithful, putting me into the ministry (1 Tim. 1:12).

Just as God prepared the place, He also prepared the man. The ancient petition, "Give us men to match our mountains," was granted in the person of Bernard Washington Spilman. God called B. W. Spilman, a man of rare vision and unbending faith, to develop the mountain of faith.

When the first train climbed the mountain and entered the Swannanoa Valley from the east in October 1880, God already was at work preparing the man who would carry the awesome responsibility of developing the mountain of faith. Spilman, named Bernard Hardee, was born Sunday, January 22, 1871. Following his father's death, Spilman took his father's middle name "Washington" as a tribute of his love for his father.[1]

That same year, Spilman accepted Jesus as his personal Savior. Christ became the inspiration for his life of dedicated service. Many times his faith was challenged, but those challenges only caused him to reach higher to serve Christ the only way he knew—"full speed ahead." Spilman, in a moment of dedication and commitment, crossed the word *failure* out of his dictionary. At the same time, he crossed it out of his life. Only then was he prepared to meet the mountain.

The vision of Ridgecrest began to develop as early as 1895 as

Spilman pondered the idea of a summer place for Southern Baptists "to meet and to learn how to teach the Bible to the multitudes." He carried the dream for the five years he served as Sunday School secretary for the Baptist Convention of North Carolina. His dream was not simply a human vision; it was a revelation from God. That dream had to find fulfillment.

Many of the challenges Spilman faced in his early ministry were times of special training he would need later.

Without the support of a broad-based Sunday School program, Ridgecrest would not become a reality. Through the years, Spilman labored to overcome apathy and antagonism, while promoting and building Sunday Schools. During the discouraging days of 1897, even the corresponding secretary of the North Carolina Baptist Convention recommended that Spilman give up. He suggested that Spilman's type of Sunday School was not being accepted. Nevertheless, Spilman continued. He laid a foundation of methods and principles on which we still build Sunday Schools. This Sunday School program became the catalyst for the development, growth, and maturity of Ridgecrest Conference Center.

During those years, Spilman also was responsible for the Sunday School Supply Store (later called the Baptist Book Store). This responsibility caused him to realize his need for a better understanding of business principles and methods. He enrolled in the Reverend J. A. Campbell's Academy at Buies Creek, North Carolina. Spilman completed the commercial course in two months. This training became another valuable asset sorely needed in a commercial venture such as Ridgecrest.

Each of the five years that he served as Sunday School secretary of North Carolina, Spilman conducted mass meetings called Mountain Chautauquas. Attendance reached 2,000 per week. This too was training for developing Ridgecrest. It also convinced Spilman that a nationwide gathering of people for Sunday School work was urgently needed.

Again and again obstacles became tools with which Spilman cultivated a life of faith and determination, traits that captured the hearts of people across the nation. His view of an obstacle is expressed in the words of William Lyon Phelps: "One man finds an obstacle a stumbling block; another finds it a stepping-stone."

Spilman consistently converted obstacles into stepping-stones. Some obstacles even became God's call to enlarged responsibilities. One of Jesus' parables concludes with the promise, "Thou hast been faithful over a few things, I will make thee ruler over many things" (Matt. 25:23). In the spirit of this passage, Spilman accepted the offer of Dr. J. M. Frost to be the first field secretary for the Sunday School Board. On June 1, 1901, Spilman began this new work, which brought him still closer to seeing his cherished dream fulfilled.

The traits that Frost saw in Spilman are the traits that made him into the man who would face the mountain. C. Sylvester Green recorded, "In Spilman Dr. Frost saw a man who had proved that he had the courage to launch a new program against tremendous odds—and opposition—and carry it through, even at great personal sacrifice."[2] Green quoted Frost, "He had both academic and theological training. He had a background of pastoral experience. He possessed unique platform ability; and his humor often disarmed opposition and opened closed doors."[3]

The years of preparation were complete and the time had arrived for the man to meet the mountain. The road was not a direct path. It wound across Tennessee and North Carolina. In 1902, a site near Fountain City, Tennessee, just outside of Knoxville was considered. Although the site's outward appearance seemed ideal, the results were disappointing to Spilman; and the search continued.

Spilman's quest led him to Chattanooga, Tennessee; Waynesville and Hendersonville, North Carolina; and then to Mars Hill. There Spilman considered a site called "Little Mountain." As much as Spilman loved Mars Hill, God was leading him to the "Big Mountain."

Finally on August 4, 1906, Bernard Washington Spilman stepped from the eastbound train at Terrell, North Carolina. For the first time he viewed the majestic mountain in all its untouched beauty. The man and the mountain would fulfill a vision and glorify the Creator as few have ever done.

"How beautiful upon the mountains are the feet of him that bringeth good tidings, that publisheth peace; that bringeth good tidings of good, that publisheth salvation; that sayeth unto Zion, Thy God reigneth!" (Isa. 52:7).

---

[1] For a fuller account of the life of Spilman, the reader is referred to C. Sylvester Green, *B. W. Spilman: The Sunday School Man* (Nashville: Broadman Press, 1953).
[2] Ibid., 59.
[3] Ibid.

3 Claiming the Mountain

Now faith is the substance of things hoped for, the evidence of things not seen (Heb. 11:1).

Four men and a small boy shared Dr. Spilman's first visit to Ridgecrest. Spilman never enjoyed working alone. His love for people and his devotion to the Lord's work caused him to share his vision and dreams with all who would listen. He was equally willing to share the responsibilities and glories with those who would share his dream. His life echoed the words of John Wesley: "If thy heart be as my heart, give me thy hand."

The first small group of visitors was composed of Spilman; James H. Tucker; Dr. Henry W. Battle of Kinston, North Carolina; Rev. William Lunsford, pastor of the First Baptist Church, Asheville, North Carolina; Landrum P. Leavell, the second Sunday School field secretary for the Sunday School Board; and Lunsford's son, Gordon.

The group spent most of the day searching out the land. They looked for and found abundant water supplies. They looked for an adequate building site in the dense forest.

In a newspaper article in 1941, Spilman reminisced about this first visit:

> Marvelous view! We strolled west leaving the railroad track and came to a spot where Pritchell Hall, the large assembly hotel, is now located. We found a small stream and followed it to its source (now Johnson Spring). Then we climbed the hill west and found an old fence of rotten rails. It was already broken in places. All the party climbed over. I, as usual weighing 260 pounds, came last. I climbed the fence. When I was

well balanced on top of the fence every rail except the bottom one broke. It was a fairly good show.[1]

Henry Battle took the lead in the first dedication service. After removing his hat and delivering a "bit of an oration," he closed by saying, "Let's buy the land and locate the first hotel on that ridge over there." With the decision in their hearts and a broken fence rail marking the spot, they returned to Asheville to begin the work of converting dreams into reality.

The site was ideal for reasons other than its beauty, climate, and natural resources. It was within reach of multitudes of Baptists. Spilman saw Ridgecrest as the center of Baptist work. In *Sunday School Young People and Adults* for June 1934, he wrote: "If a circle, with a radius of 500 miles was inscribed, with Ridgecrest as a center, the rim of the circle would touch approximately New York, Chicago, Little Rock, New Orleans, and cross the peninsula of Florida about half-way between Jacksonville and Key West. Within the circle would be the capitals of 18 states."

Spilman knew in his heart that he had found the place. He also knew that Baptists had to be led, not pushed. They would have to find Ridgecrest in their own way. In December 1906, he presented the concept of an assembly to the North Carolina Baptist State Convention. He asked the people of North Carolina to locate the assembly in their state and to invite others to join them in a cooperative development effort.

In a resolution passed by the convention, a committee was to be appointed; but it was understood that the convention would assume no financial responsibility. The committee included three of the first visitors: James Tucker, Henry Battle, and Spilman. In addition, Needham B. Broughton and Hight C. Moore were asked to serve. At the time Broughton was part owner of the *Biblical Recorder*, which remains today the North Carolina Baptist paper. Moore became a field secretary in charge of teacher training for the Sunday School Board in 1907.

The members of this committee easily could go back to the site that had captivated their hearts and minds. In fact, Spilman revealed later that he had obtained options on the land with faith that he could persuade Baptists to build an assembly "which would be the equal of any assembly in the world."

The original 940 acres were purchased by the committee. Spilman reported that this purchase was the first step in the development of "The Southern Baptist Assembly."

Spillman reported: "Entering into correspondence and by personal visits to many in other states, it seemed that time was at hand for such a move. Accordingly, without waiting for any further action by the North Carolina Baptist State Convention and without reporting to that Convention the committee secured a charter from the general assembly of North Carolina."[2]

The act to incorporate "The Southern Baptist Assembly" was ratified March 8, 1907, in the state legislature at Raleigh. The purpose stated in the charter was: "To establish and maintain in the mountains of Western North Carolina a municipality of Baptist Assemblies, convention conferences, public worship, missionary and school work, orphan homes, manual and teachers training and other operations auxiliary and incidental thereto: also a religion resort with permanent and temporary dwellings, for health, rest, recreation, cluster work and fellowship."[3]

The charter provided for a mayor, town marshal, tax collector, treasurer, and "other officers," all appointed by the Board of Directors. The original committee served as the unofficial Board of Directors until a Board could be elected.

Two important endorsements of the committee's actions were received that first year. The Southern Baptist Convention meeting in its 1907 annual session in Richmond, Virginia, passed the following resolution in reference to the Western North Carolina Assembly: "At the request of the North Carolina Baptist State Convention, the Southern Baptist Convention does hereby endorse the movement without assuming any financial responsibility."[4]

The second endorsement was the first official participation of the Sunday School Board. Spilman proposed to resign from the Board to devote full time to the new assembly. J. M. Frost preferred to share in the work by allowing Spilman to carry out his assembly responsibilities and remain a field consultant for the Board. He gave Spilman total freedom in scheduling his work between the two ministries. None of his time was to be charged to the assembly.

Frost foresaw the tremendous contribution that Ridgecrest would make to Sunday School work. His wisdom and insight were the beginning of a relationship that has continued to make Ridgecrest possible through the years. Without the Sunday School Board, Ridgecrest probably would have passed from the scene during the early years of its development.

In the summer of 1907, the Board of Directors asked Spilman to become the project's general manager and to accept responsibility for leading the development process. He began his official work as general manager September 1, 1907.

The Sunday School Board purchased one parcel of land for $8,507.80. An additional $1,801.19 was spent on surveys and other actions necessary to complete the sale. The "man" now owned the mountain. Spilman's dream was a reality. Faith drew a vision; faith filled the hearts of these men of God; and faith claimed the mountain.

---

[1] Cited by R. L. Middleton, *A Dream Come True* (Nashville: Broadman Press, 1957), 11–12.

[2] In 1928 Bernard Spilman delivered a challenging report to the annual meeting of the Board of Directors. He outlined the past history, the current condition, and his view of the future. The stockholders later printed the speech for circulation. See Bernard W. Spilman, *Ridgecrest: Past, Present, Future* (Asheville: Jarrett's Press, Inc., 1928) for the text of the report. Hereinafter referred to as President's Address, 1928.

[3] Charter of the Southern Baptist Assembly, executed March 8, 1907.

[4] *Southern Baptist Convention Annual*, 1907, 33.

4. Financing the Mountain

For which of you, intending to build a tower, sitteth not down first, and counteth the cost, whether he have sufficient to finish it? (Luke 14:28).

The North Carolina Baptist State Convention had empowered the committee but provided no financial assistance. The full burden of financing the project fell on the committee as it prepared to move forward.

In order to plan carefully the development and to provide adequate financing, Spilman opened a temporary office in Asheville September 2, 1907. A loan secured from the Battery Park Bank in Asheville in the amount of $3,000 was crucial to his plan. He soon raised an additional $14,000 from the sale of lots and stock.

Spilman believed the "mountain" could support itself. He engaged C. D. Beadle of Pittsburgh, Pennsylvania, to survey and plot the land. Beadle was well known as the surveyor and designer of the Biltmore Estates in Asheville.

According to the early maps, the area was divided into over 800 plots. Each plot was approximately one-half acre in size and was accessible by automobile. This foresight was remarkable, considering that the first automobile to scale the mountain and enter Swannanoa Valley from the east arrived two years later in 1909.

The property layout was a masterpiece of engineering. Elevation varied from 2,500 feet to 3,225 feet. Spilman often accompanied the engineers. He later related one of his trips in a newspaper article.

"One day with one of the young engineers as a guide, Mr. Tucker, Mr. H. B. Craven, who owned some adjoining land, and I rode horseback over the boundary trail of the entire property. The trip required about one half a day and was the roughest ride I ever expect to have. We went up mountainsides, down into valleys, through jungles and briars, and on and on we went. When we were through with it the horse which I rode, I am sure, was never the same again; and I was not for many weeks. I do not recall that I have been horseback riding since."[1]

The lots were sold for $100 and included one share of stock. A few persons bought stock for $100, foregoing any claim to the land. Stock was limited to 500 shares, which put a ceiling on the number of stockholders.

An endowment brochure published in 1911 listed three Southern Baptist Boards among the stockholders. The Foreign Mission Board, the Home Mission Board, and the Sunday School Board had become stockholders through gifts from friends. These friends felt that the Boards should have a vote in the control of the assembly's affairs. They purchased the stock and donated it to the three agencies. Many Baptist colleges and Baptist state papers also held stock.

All of the survey work was completed by the fall of 1907, and the $14,000 soon was raised in cash and pledged purchases. The lot sales, stock sales, and the loan put the assembly in business without obligating funds from any Convention agency.

On May 21, 1907, the original committee called the stockholders together to organize the corporation formally. The meeting was held under an apple tree in the yard of the Old Stage Coach Inn. This committee elected the first Board of Directors with James H. Tucker as chairman.

The directors were elected with the understanding that the corporation was a trust for Southern Baptist. Resolutions were passed later by the board and by the annual stockholders meeting certifying that all property, funds, and goodwill were not for private profit. These were held in trust for Baptist people and their friends.

With the land secured and the corporation organized, construction began June 11, 1908. Utilizing an abandoned camp used by railroad engineers during construction of the railroad, the craftsmen set up headquarters at the "Dew-Drop-Inn."

The matter of a name for the assembly was becoming a problem. The name "Terrell" had been changed to "Blue Mont" to reflect the majesty of the Blue Ridge Mountains. This created problems for the railroad because their shorthand code for Blue Mont was the same as for Black Mountain. It took some time to find just the right name for the assembly. Many were considered. C. S. Green reported the final agreement: "Now and then a new name was suggested, but none seemed to be the right one. One night Spilman, mulling over names, thought of calling it Ridgecrest, for it was just that—the crest of high ridge, and the railway station was one of the highest east of the Rockies. The very next morning he met Hight C. Moore. "Good morning," said Dr. Moore. "Mrs. Moore has just thought of a name for the assembly. What do you think of calling it Ridgecrest?"[2]

They immediately agreed that Ridgecrest was a splendid choice.

During the remainder of 1908 and 1909, Spilman was aided greatly by E. L. Hon of Deland, Florida. Hon, an astute businessman and a member of the board of directors, provided invaluable business judgment. He donated his services and established sound operational principles, which the assembly could follow for the years ahead.

In September 1909, the responsibilities of leadership were divided to provide a more effective organization. Spilman was named general secretary and given responsibility for all legal affairs. Hon served as general manager and was given responsibility for the grounds and facilities.

A separate accounting of funds was kept for each phase of the ministry. The general manager's fund included income from the sale of lots, corporation taxes, services rendered, and gifts for improvements. Expenses for the salary of the general manager, care of the grounds and building, construction of roads, and matters related to the grounds and buildings were paid from this fund.

The general secretary's fund included income from summer program fees, offerings, and gifts from churches and individuals. Expenses included costs of the summer program, advertising, and other miscellaneous matters. The railroad provided advertising assistance. The Sunday School Board continued to provide salary assistance for the general secretary. Seven months of his salary was charged to the assembly, and the Board paid the other five months plus all travel expenses.

This arrangement allowed the assembly to operate without a

deficit for at least the first 20 years. The shared manager arrangement was so effective that it was maintained for the life of the corporation. Spilman reported in 1929 on the stewardship of these early stockholders, saying:

> Thus came into being the splendid property which in due time was given to the Southern Baptists as represented by the Southern Baptist Convention to be held in trust for all time for the glory of God and the advancement of His kingdom. Never a dollar of dividend was declared to any stockholder beyond the lot which he secured at the time that he took stock. During all the years when the property was held by the corporation the owners kept faith with the folk and not a dollar from any source ever found its way into the pocket of any stockholder as a dividend on his investment.[3]

Spilman further reported "that the fund of the general secretary never showed at the close of the season a deficit of a single cent." No one will ever know how much personal money Spilman gave to bring about that balance. He never spoke of his own contributions.

A newspaper article that appeared in 1936 revealed numerous acts of philanthropy that Spilman generously performed during his lifetime. A nine-room house, which he built for his own personal use, and at least six other lots were included among his gifts to the assembly. He gave another nine-room house on the assembly grounds to the North Carolina Convention for their use at the assembly.

The assembly and Board of Directors would face several financial crises in the years ahead. Spilman himself declared "that only the hand of God saved the assembly from becoming a lost cause." The ever-empowering faith of these men kept step with the leadership of God on the mountain of faith.

---

[1] Cited from a newspaper article by Middleton, *A Dream Come True*, 61–62.
[2] Green, *B. W. Spilman*, 90.
[3] President's Address, 1928.

5 Testing Their Faith

But we glory in tribulations also: knowing that the tribulation worketh patience; and patience, experience; and experience, hope (Rom. 5:3-4).

From the morning of June 11, 1908, when construction began, until the evening of August 4, 1920, many crises tested those who were dedicated to building the assembly. On August 4, the Education Board of the Southern Baptist Convention was given 248 shares of stock, allowing it to assume controlling interest. That actualized Spilman's dream that the assembly would belong to all Southern Baptists.

The 12 intervening years were a mixture of joy and tears. These were years that required men to bend their backs in labor and their knees in prayer. It seemed that each time their goal was within reach another crisis created a setback. These men believed that they were developing God's mountain for His people, according to His will. That faith was tested often, but it never failed. Spilman's deletion of the word *failure* from his dictionary was characteristic of every person involved. No one even considered quitting.

"The struggle of the next four years to keep out of the hands of the sheriff, if written, would read like a romance."[1] These words spoken during an annual report to the Board of Directors were later recorded in written form. This speech and other documents fortunately captured much of the romance, a romance of bitter and sweet, joy and sorrow, exaltation and depression.

Personal tragedy was the first crisis. In the summer of 1908, Spilman's young daughter died. Only a few weeks old, Agnes Mozelle seemed to foreshadow the peaks of joy and the valleys of heartbreak that Spilman would face.

The first summer program was conducted in 1909. The new

auditorium was completed for public services. An estimated crowd of 600 attended the first service in the auditorium.

The success of the summer programs caused the Board of Directors to vote to issue bonds for the erection of a hotel. Later the board chose to borrow $10,000 from Jefferson Standard Life Insurance Company of Greensboro, North Carolina, rather than to sell bonds. Ground breaking ceremonies were held August 12, 1911.

Shadows of sorrow again fell on February 15, 1912, with the death of James Tucker. Spilman's dependence on the aid of this faithful servant is reflected in his tribute to him (see "Tributes" at the end of this book). Judge C. Pritchard was elected to replace Tucker as chairman of the Board of Directors.

By the fall of 1913, the Board of Directors realized that financial conditions had become serious. The directors agreed in annual session to obtain a $35,000 loan in order to consolidate their indebtedness. The loan was to be secured by a second mortgage on the property. The board was unable to locate a lender willing to accept the collateral. This lack of capital and the outstanding debts significantly delayed plans. Perhaps the most serious setback was the delay in construction of the new hotel.

Early 1914 brought a new ray of hope. Judge Pritchard was able to negotiate a loan for $20,000. Old Dominion Trust Company of Richmond, Virginia, agreed to finance the debt through a bond issue. The assurance of this financing allowed construction of the hotel to begin. J. D. Elliott of Hickory, North Carolina, a member of the Executive Committee, was enlisted as the contractor. He provided his services without charge as a contribution to the assembly.

On March 1, 1914, disaster struck again. This time the dark cloud came in the form of a terrific windstorm that destroyed the auditorium built in 1909. Considering the impact of the loss to the assembly, it is no wonder that Spilman later referred to the storm as a hurricane. Fortunately, Fidelis Hall had just been completed in November 1912 and was used as a temporary auditorium.

The joy of watching the new hotel rise from the foundation and take shape held back the clouds of depression. The financial picture was not improving, but the assurance of the bond issue kept the work moving. By midsummer the new hotel was nearing completion.

Judge Pritchard had negotiated the loan and spent a great deal of time soliciting funds to keep the assembly alive. Elliott led the construction crews and made significant contributions toward the construction of the hotel. In their honor, Pritchard's and Elliott's names were joined to name the hotel Pritchell Inn. The name was changed later to Pritchell Hall.

On July 28, 1914, the hotel was ready. The furniture was being put in place. Spilman sat in the offices of Old Dominion Trust Company signing the bonds. News arrived that war had erupted in Europe. The beginning of World War I rocked the nation, and Old Dominion withdrew the bonds, leaving the assembly with all the debts outstanding.

In the midst of the crisis, faith stood strong. Pritchell Inn officially opened on August 1, 1914. Each room in the fine new structure was equipped with a private bowl and pitcher. Many early residents carried water from Johnson Spring. The new hotel included bedrooms, kitchen, dining room, and auditorium space.

Four guests enjoyed dinner that first evening. Spilman was joined by Judge and Mrs. Pritchard and A. L. Boyd of Charlotte, North Carolina. They dined without the benefit of the electric lights which were not connected for several days.

Joseph P. Wilson served as host. Arrangements had been made to lease the operation of the hotel to Wilson on a percentage of income basis. The hotel was expected to generate enough income to cover all of its operating expenses. However, a significant increase in total guests would be required to make the hotel profitable. With the 1914 season almost over, income from the hotel would be delayed until the summer of 1915.

The summer of 1915 brought more financial problems. These difficulties were compounded by Spilman's illness. He spent most of the summer under the care of his physician. By the time of the August Board of Directors meeting, the assembly debts exceeded $32,000. No outside financing seemed to be available. Some of the Executive Committee members signed personal notes, allowing a few of the smaller debts to be paid. This left unpaid a $2,000 debt owed to the Parker-Gardner Company of Charlotte, North Carolina, for hotel furnishings.

C. W. Tillett, Jr., a lawyer for Parker-Gardner, approached Spilman in August with a demand for immediate payment. The directors, in emergency session, offered to sign a note guaranteeing the debt in full. Tillett refused and affirmed his intention to file suit immediately.

The directors averted this disaster by swift action. They agreed to sell all unmortgaged property to Spilman in settlement of a $1,400 loan that also was due. Arrangements were made by J. D. Moore for the Clerk of Courts in Asheville, North Carolina, to remain open until Spilman could arrive to record the transfer. George Emmett of New Bern, North Carolina, was paid $4.50 to carry Spilman to Asheville in an automobile.

Tillett had to wait for the next train to Asheville, which removed any possibility of his filing suit that day. On his arrival the next morning, the Clerk of Court explained that the assembly did not own enough to make a suit worthwhile. Spilman owned the property, but he had no obligation to Parker-Gardner. Spilman held the title until 1919, when all debts had been paid. He then deeded the property back to the assembly.

The board was anxious to assure Parker-Gardner that the debt would be cleared. While Spilman was on his way to Asheville, another director left by train for Charlotte. N. B. Josey delivered a signed note to cover the total indebtedness. The note was paid in full.

The summer of 1916 was hindered by the greatest flood in the history of the area. The Southern Railway tracks, which scaled the mountain from Old Fort, were washed out. Consequently, almost all traffic from the east came to a stop. The highway from Asheville was washed away, halting traffic from the west. Programming and attendance were reduced severely.

A new school of theology was scheduled to begin that summer. Dr. C. B. Williams was the only faculty member to arrive. In order to meet his responsibilities, he walked over 40 miles, carrying his suitcase.

Adding to the discouragement, Pritchell Hall was still operating at a loss. Many private homes and rooming houses had been built during the hotel's construction. With the other hindrances holding down attendance, the hotel could not earn enough income to offset operating expenses.

The overall debt load was staggering. In 1918, the interest charge on the debt was greater than the income generated by the assembly. Program contributions from the Sunday School Board and the Home Mission Board plus some individual contributions allowed the programs to be conducted for 1916, 1917, and 1918.

The Board of Directors felt that Pritchell Hall had to be sold as a means of liquidating the debt. For months the building remained for sale at an extremely favorable price. No buyers could be located. One offer was made, and a down payment was accepted; but the buyer was unable to follow through. Spilman later credited the hand of God with saving the assembly by not allowing Pritchell Hall to be sold.

The board decided to take the hotel off the market and use the facility for assembly headquarters. In addition, Spilman decided to launch a nationwide drive to raise $100,000. One-half of these funds would be used to liquidate debts and to make capital improvements. The remainder would be used as an endowment fund.

The financial picture had been aggravated during these years by a continuous change of business managers. From E. L. Hon's one year of service in 1910, six different men served as business managers over the first 10-year period. This instability in business management was felt most drastically in the inability to raise funds. Spilman was forced to give less and less time to fund raising as his other responsibilities continued to grow.

On January 1, 1919, the directors employed Dr. Livingston T. Mays as corresponding secretary. His primary responsibilities were to raise the $100,000 and to assume the summer platform management. Later, he also became business manager.

Spilman credited Mays with turning the assembly around financially. Under his leadership attendance grew rapidly. Funds came in as people responded to May's call to assist. Most amazing of all, Mays was able to reduce the floating debt that had lingered so long.

Mays had to face some dark moments. Just as the financial

picture appeared to be on the road to recovery, another crisis emerged. The Jefferson Standard Life Insurance Company requested immediate settlement of its loan. The loan obtained in 1911 was secured by a property mortgage. The interest had been paid, but the principle had not been reduced in the eight-year period. The full $10,000 was required to settle the debt. The Commonwealth Bank and Trust Company of Black Mountain rescued the assembly on that occasion. A loan was negotiated, and Jefferson Standard was paid in full.

With the $100,000 campaign under way, the assembly again could see a bright future. Pledges and subscriptions in the amount of $40,000 had been committed. A major portion of the funds came from North Carolina Baptists, exceeding the convention request for North Carolina churches to raise $20,000 of the $100,000 goal.

The Southern Baptist Convention, meeting in Atlanta in 1919, launched the $75 million campaign for all purposes in the South except local church expenses. The assembly was not officially an agency of the Convention, but it did not seem wise for the two campaigns to be conducted at the same time. Spilman asked that the assembly be included in the $75 million campaign. The conditions of inclusion were not at all favorable to the assembly. However, the great desire "to keep step with our Baptist brothers" and a desire "to be a part of the Baptist movement" caused the Board of Directors to agree to the terms, which included:

1. The assembly would cancel all unpaid pledges. The North Carolina Baptist State Convention donated $20,000 in lieu of over $40,000 in pledges.

2. The assembly would withdraw from any direct appeals to the churches and be a part of the campaign.

3. The assembly would go under the direction of the Education Board of the Southern Baptist Convention.

4. The assembly would receive 1/60th of the annual amount of the $75 million campaign given the Education Board.

The maximum contribution the assembly could expect to receive was $50,000 over five years. The offsetting factor would be the security provided by being a part of a Southern Baptist Convention agency. Also, the knowledge that the assembly would belong to all

Southern Baptists was important. This was part of Spilman's original dream and purpose.

Spilman felt that under this new arrangement the assembly would be on a solid financial basis. Most of the indebtedness had been paid by 1920. He resigned his position with the assembly to give more of his time to his Sunday School Board responsibilities.

The Board of Directors maintained the corporation in order to continue to do business in North Carolina. The directors held the founding charter so they could assume responsibility for the assembly if conditions ever required their services. The charter was surrendered in 1934 when the total operation was transferred to the Sunday School Board.

Hight C. Moore summarized those stormy years in these words:

Rainbows over Ridgecrest

It takes the mountains to furnish the most picturesque setting for a thunderstorm. There is the element of warfare, of struggle, of heroic conquest. The clouds plunge, but the peaks stand; the lightning leaps and occasionally strikes, but the forest loses a giant and abides; the thunder deafens and startles, but the mountains toss it back and forth to each other as players throw the ball from base to base on a diamond; the knolls and ridges and valleys nestle the while securely among the great mountains even as little chickens under the wings of a hen in time of storm. What is more majestic?

But, after the storm, the bow in the cloud; after the double rainbow, the ineffable sunset; and after the sunset, the stars stud the sky with such distinctness and nearness that you almost reach out your hand to touch them—all reminding us of showers of blessing and rainbows of promise and stars of direction that vouchsafe for Ridgecrest glory and greatness in the purposes of God.[2]

---

[1] President's Address, 1928.
[2] Moore, *The Story of Ridgecrest*, 25.

⑥ Programming by Faith

Give instruction to a wise man, and he will be yet wiser. Teach a just man, and he will increase in learning (Prov. 9:9).

Programs always have been the heart of the assembly. All other activities support this primary function. The purpose of the assembly was not to build buildings, erect monuments, or to establish a resort. The purpose always was envisioned as an educational experience, a time of training and learning to endow church members with the ability to serve better in their churches. The place ideally suited for such an experience was Ridgecrest.

The first worship service at Ridgecrest was an unofficial service of thanksgiving conducted on the front porch of James Tucker's cabin. Following the formal incorporation meeting on May 21, 1908, several of the group moved to Tucker's cabin. Spilman led the service and preached the first sermon at Ridgecrest. Six persons attended this first assembly.

The oak fireplace from Tucker's cabin has been preserved. A plaque commemorating this beginning service was mounted in the fireplace in 1948. The fireplace stands today as a memorial to those men and their vision.

The first official program was in the summer of 1909. The first auditorium was ready in time for the summer activities. The building was more of a tabernacle than an auditorium. It featured homemade benches, a sawdust floor, and only one enclosed side.

The first service was held on July 19, 1909, and was attended by approximately 600 people. Hight C. Moore delivered the first sermon, entitled "Christ on the Cross." A highlight of the first summer's program was the Sunday worship services held each week for the full seven-week season. The preachers represented a wide cross section of Southern Baptist life. The denomination was represented by: Livingston Johnson, corresponding secretary of the Southern Baptist Layman's Movement; T. B. Ray, education secretary of the Foreign Mission Board; J. L. White, H. W. Battle, J. D. Moore, and pastors from North Carolina; W. W. Hamilton, pastor from Virginia, and E. C. Dargan, pastor from Georgia.

The summer had three main program periods:

July 18–August 1: Sunday School, Baptist Young People's Union, and Mission Conference

July 30–31: Layman's Conference

August 8–22: Bible Conference

Measured by today's standards or by other mass meetings of that day, Ridgecrest was small, and the program was limited. The total program cost for the summer was $400. The number of faculty was limited, and the attendance was not great. But it was a beginning. A dream had been realized, and the purposes as stated by Spilman had been fulfilled:

> It was the purpose of the founders to make the assembly grounds a gathering place where Baptists might meet throughout the summer months to discuss in a quiet, restful, congenial, spiritual atmosphere their problems—problems of missions, Sunday School and Baptist Young People's Union work, Christian education, social service, Bible study, and such other things as came within the realm of the thinking of God on earth.[1]

The following printed program for 1910 summarized adequately the program content, philosophy of charges, and the basic operating concepts of the assembly leadership.

Cost of Admission to the Auditorium

During the summer of 1910, admission to the grounds will be free. An admission fee will be charged to all exercises in the Auditorium except the services on Sunday, the Get Acquainted Socials on Tuesday and the B.Y.P.U. Socials, which may be given during the summer.

Tickets may be purchased at the Blue Mont Store or at the

entrance to the Auditorium. The prices are as follows:

Single admission, good for 24 hours	0.25
Two days	0.50
One week	1.00
Two weeks	2.00
Season	3.00
Season ticket, good for family (two persons)	4.50
Each additional person in the family	1.00
Children 15 years and under	Free

The Emphasis by Weeks

Each week of the season a certain phase of the work will be emphasized. The addresses of the morning will be along the line of the work receiving emphasis for the week. This generally will be true of the evening addresses. The following schedule will be observed:

July 10–15: Sunday School and B.Y.P.U
July 17–22: Mission and the Layman's Movement
July 24–29: Education
July 31–August 5: Music and Athletics
August 7–21: Bible Conference

An additional feature of the 1910 program was the opening of a school of religious education. Five faculty members were enlisted, but only Spilman and Dr. George W. Green arrived and participated. Green observed, "The program proceeded as if there had been 600." In addition to two classroom periods each day, platform addresses were delivered at 11:00 a.m. and 8:00 p.m.

In spite of the financial difficulties and trying times of the early years, attendance grew as the summer programs improved year after year. With the opening of Pritchell Hall in 1914, a new attendance record was realized. Twenty states were represented with a total attendance of 1,286 for the summer.

In 1916, a summer school of theology was launched. The school was to run concurrently with the other programs. The assembly planned to have a quality faculty and a program that would be accredited by all the seminaries. However, the flood of 1916 greatly diminished the first year's potential attendance, with C. B. Williams being the only faculty member to arrive.

In 1917, The Southern Baptist Theological Seminary, Southwestern Baptist Theological Seminary, and a seminary connected to Mercer University gave full credit for the courses completed at the Ridgecrest School of Theology. The school never realized the level of achievement Spilman desired. In 1928, he reported that "the Summer School of Theology has been a feature with varying fortunes since the summer of 1916."

The years from 1915 to 1918 were drastically affected by financial difficulties. The Sunday School Board and the Home Mission Board made it possible to conduct programs during these summers.

Spilman reported to the Board of Directors at their 1918 meeting the Sunday School Board's contribution to the assembly. At the same time, he called for more support from other Convention agencies:

> The Boards of the Southern Baptist Convention should get behind this assembly. The Sunday School Board has helped in ways almost beyond number. This year, in addition to furnishing the services of one of its Field Secretaries to be General Secretary of the Assembly, the Sunday School Board has made a cash contribution larger than the total amount contributed for the program by all other [agencies] thus far this summer. The Sunday School Board is willing, even anxious, to help those who help themselves, but the Board is not going to continue to aid where the people who receive the benefit do not care for their part of the work. Dr. Van Ness, the corresponding secretary of the Sunday School Board, is going to recommend . . . that the Board care for the total expense of a high grade summer school for Christian workers during the summer of 1919.[2]

Spilman turned back to North Carolina Baptists, requesting that Ridgecrest be granted a gift equal to what North Carolina Baptists budgeted for their own assembly. The state board of missions granted Ridgecrest $5,000 for the summer of 1920. Small contributions from individual friends of the assembly continued to supplement these larger gifts.

Spilman was deeply appreciative of the Home Mission Board's and the Sunday School Board's efforts and was eternally grateful for the donations of close friends. He still felt, however, that the assembly was not receiving adequate support for its programs. His personal burden and disappointment are reflected in words delivered to the Board of Directors in an annual report: "Our present financial plan and program for the General Secretary's Department seems to me to be about as near a failure as a thing could to exist at all. . . . The pitifully inadequate amount provided by the voluntary contributions is enough to make us think that the Southern Baptist Assembly is engaged in a peanut stand business in the realm of assemblies."[3]

With the Education Board's acceptance of financial responsibility for the center in 1920, programming responsibilities also were transferred to that agency.

Program benefits cannot be measured by immediate results. The balance sheet cannot be totaled at the end of the season. Reports cannot be gathered as to the benefits of 2,500 people dispersed back to the churches in 19 states. However, the reports received and the visible results during the programs were enough to keep hope alive and spirits dreaming of brighter days ahead.

The cornerstone installed when the main auditorium was enlarged in 1953 reflects the value of this programming effort: "From the mountaintop of vision Southern Baptists would carry the message of Christ into every valley of human need."

---

[1] President's Address, 1928.
[2] Middleton, *A Dream Come True*, 22.
[3] Minutes of the Board of Directors, August 7, 1918.

7 The Education Board Years

Take heed to the ministry which thou has received in the Lord, that thou fulfill it (Col. 4:17).

The Education Board assumed full responsibility for the Southern Baptist assembly in 1920. On August 4 of that year, the stockholders transferred 248 shares of stock to the Education Board. This stock plus the three shares already held by the Home Mission, Foreign Mission, and Sunday School Boards gave the Southern Baptist Convention controlling interest with 251 shares. The charter provided that no more than 500 shares could be issued. Since the full 500 shares had never been issued, this action actually gave the Education Board absolute control of the assembly.

The Board of Directors deeded all the land, buildings, furnishing, and cash assets to the Education Board. Spilman reported that the debt at the time was $9,071.86. This was made up mostly of miscellaneous accounts.

The Education Board was scheduled to receive $3 million from the $75 million campaign. According to the agreements previously mentioned, Ridgecrest was to share in the Education Board's part of that $3 million. The 1920 report of the Education Board to the Southern Baptist Convention stated: "Relative to the Southern Baptist Assembly at Ridgecrest . . . after thorough investigation, it was decided that at least $100,000 was needed to care for this institution, but the funds at our disposal permitted us to appropriate only $50,000 to be prorated and paid out of the $3,000,000 fund, the same as other southwide institutions."[1]

Dr. Albert R. Bond, editorial secretary of the Education Board, assumed responsibility for summer programming. In addition to his other duties, he served as general manger and general secretary of the assembly. With no one giving full time to the assembly, little could be done by way of development and expansion. In addition, a shortage of funds continued to plague the operation.

The internal financial plan had been changed from Spilman's pattern of separate funds for programs and facilities. Under the Board's management, the earnings of the hotel were to pay all the expenses of the program. If this source of revenue failed, the additional amount was to come out of the allocation made from the $75 million campaign. With the hotel failing to generate the additional income, funds previously expected for capital improvements were used for programming.

The $75 million campaign never reached the total contributions expected by its promoters. When the campaign closed, Ridgecrest had received less than half of the projected $50,000. Actual receipts given to the assembly from the campaign totaled only $23,319.82. Obligations and expenses for this same period were $32,024.30. The Education Board had to contribute $10,357.30 of its operating funds to the operating budget of Ridgecrest in 1922 and 1923.

Frustration concerning the assembly operation can be sensed in the 1923 report for the Education Board to the Southern Baptist Convention: "Your committee urges Southern Baptists to realize the possibilities of the Southern Baptist Assembly at Ridgecrest, North Carolina, eighteen miles beyond Asheville, unsurpassed for its climatic advantages and scenic beauty . . ideal for a summer assembly of national scope and power."[2]

Dr. W. C. James, corresponding secretary of the Education Board, resigned in July 1924. Dr. J. W. Cammack was elected as his successor, effective October 1, 1924. Cammack sensed the need for his personal attention to be given to Ridgecrest and immediately took an active part in its administration. He maintained an office at Ridgecrest during the summer months. In this way, he felt he could better observe the assembly's needs firsthand and be better prepared to find ways of meeting those needs.

The desire to have more direct leadership at Ridgecrest led to a most unusual resolution being presented to the 1925 Southern Baptist Convention. It recommended that the Convention move the Education Board's headquarters from Birmingham, Alabama, to Asheville, North Carolina. The Committee on Resolutions asked the Convention not to approve the resolution. The idea was not pursued.

While reporting to the 1924 Convention, the Education Board pleaded for more funds for the assembly. The Board members reported that the assembly had been hampered continuously by the lack of funds. They listed special needs such as a good hotel, an auditorium, and numerous other rental facilities. They reported that the money received from the $75 million campaign had gone for payment of obligations incurred before the Board assumed responsibility for the assembly. In contrast to this statement, the 1925 report showed the $9,071.86 debt still was outstanding.

Dissatisfaction with the Education Board's operation of the assembly led to another unusual resolution being introduced in the 1924 Convention. The Baptist Pastors Conference of Asheville, North Carolina, requested that the Convention direct the Education Board to "legally and properly turn over and transfer Ridgecrest stock to the Sunday School Board, and that the Sunday School Board take charge." The resolution was referred to the Committee on Correlation with a request to report back to the Convention the following year. In 1925, the Committee on Correlation recommended "that the Education Board continue the administration of the Southern Baptist Assembly as their funds would allow."

The 1924 Convention gave some instructions to the Education Board concerning the Southern BaptistAssembly. The fifth part of a report by the Committee to Report on the Report of the Education Board was approved. It reads: "We recommend that the Convention instruct the Education Board to prepare a definite, practical schedule of its plans and needs for the development at Ridgecrest of a great summer assembly for Southern Baptists, and that there be made to it a sufficient appropriation by the committee in charge of the next campaign to properly finance the undertaking. We ought to make this enterprise worthy of our strength or abandon it. It deserves to be made a rich contribution to our Baptist life. We cannot afford to maintain it other than adequately."[3]

In response to the Convention's action and to meet the most urgent needs, in November 1924 the Education Board approved $35,000 for a multipurpose building. The structure was to contain a dining room seating 300 people, a 600-seat auditorium, and three additional classroom areas that would open into the auditorium. It also would contain a kitchen and lounge. The plans were approved on the condition that the total amount necessary to put the building in usable condition for the 1926 season would not exceed $35,000. The building that was erected was the first Rhododendron Hall. It was remodeled in 1938, and the second-floor auditorium was converted into bedrooms. This building served until it was replaced in 1967 by the present Rhododendron Hall.

In January 1925, the Education Board employed Reverend R. F. Staples as business manager of the assembly. He returned Ridgecrest to the Spilman pattern of one budget for grounds and development and a separate budget for program responsibility. In February, the Board approved a $40,000 mortgage for repairs and capital improvements. The money also was to repay the Education Board the funds it advanced to the assembly in 1922–1923. With the small amount remaining, Staples was about to erect a temporary auditorium behind Pritchell Hall and develop recreational facilities. The Education Board reported, as requested, to the 1925 Convention. The urgency of their needs and the inadequacy of funds is reflected in their report.

> The need for a new hotel and a permanent auditorium and dormitories is very urgent. Under the present financial situation, the committee on building has cut out every item that was not essential to continuing their work, and while the improvements costing $250,000 are immediately and urgently needed, the program of improvements this spring has been cut to $35,000.
>
> Because of a lack of proper conveniences and

facilities at Ridgecrest for caring for those who would have come to us, many of our people have been securing quarters at the Assembly ground of other denominations, and at the Y.M.C.A. Assembly. Our Board has approved a plan of development to begin at the earliest time possible, which consists of:
(a) A new and larger hotel
(b) A permanent auditorium
(c) Two additional dormitories
(d) Library and missionary building
(e) Several cottages
(f) Improvement of roads
(g) Light and water plant.

For these permanent improvements a million dollars might be economically and worthily invested. For a beginning of this work, we should have at least $300,000.

We have secured the advice of six non-Baptist, disinterested real estate firms that are familiar with the situation, as to the value of the present holdings of the Education Board of Ridgecrest. The figures we have accepted are lower than the lowest estimate placed on the property by only one of the six firms, and are not over 50 percent of the value placed by some of them. Present estimated value:

(a) Lots and Park Land $367,200
(b) Pritchell Hall 31,000
(c) Improvements this year 35,000
(d) Equipment 7,500
TOTAL $440,700

The total indebtedness on the property is $44,071.86. Of this amount $9,071.86 is for debts assumed by our Board when it took over the property and for improvements made prior to 1925. The balance of $35,000 represents the amount spent for necessary improvements this year.[4]

The Convention favorably received the report. It approved the development plan and authorized the Education Board to sell $300,000 in bonds to finance the plan. At that time, the Board issued only $150,000 for the first stage of construction. Of this amount, $81,501.13 was used in 1926 and $68,384.13 was used in 1927. In addition to completing Rhododendron Hall, seven small cottages, a cafeteria building, a home for the assembly manager, and several small hotel units known as "bird huts" were completed.

The assembly and the Education Board were not alone in feeling the adverse effects of fund shortages from the $75 million campaign. Several agencies had made plans and implemented programs based on projected income from the campaign. When the campaign closed and the funds had not come, many were left with outstanding obligations that could not be met from regular operating funds.

The Southern Baptist Convention had to face this critical situation when it met in Houston, Texas, for its 1926 session. The matter was resolved temporarily by the following action: "That the convention instruct the boards and activities to proceed immediately with arrangements for carrying their debts over a reasonable period if this is necessary, if by extending their obligations over a period they can be taken care of gradually without the necessity of too great curtailment in the immediate operations of these boards and activities."[5]

The Education Board immediately refinanced its indebtedness. The property was mortgaged with Real Estate Mortgage Trust Company of Saint Louis, Missouri, for the amount of $345,000. The sum of $150,000 was used to repay the previous bond issue for the 1926–1927 improvements. In late 1927 and early 1928, the Education Board had obligated the assembly for an additional $31,941.84 to build a reservoir and chlorinating plant. This debt was to be paid in seven equal payments due annually in November.

Cammack resigned his position with the Education Board in May 1927 to accept a pastorate in Danville, Virginia. He was replaced by Dr. Rufus W. Weaver July 6, 1927. Meanwhile, the dissatisfaction with the financial position of the Education Board became a concern for the Convention. The Convention's responsibility for paying the huge Education Board debt created discussion, as reflected

in the report of the Committee to Report on the Report of the Education Board. The report stated to the 1927 Convention:
> We respectfully call the Convention's attention to both its moral and legal obligation which was assumed last year when it instructed the Education Board to bond its indebtedness . . . and expressed the purpose of increasing the percentage of allocation to the Education Board in order to provide funds for the retirement of the bonds. The bonding of the indebtedness has been accomplished, and the bonds have been placed with Real Estate Mortgage Trust Company of St. Louis, Missouri, said company accepting the same on their faith in this action of the Convention. This, as we understand it, is both a moral and a legal obligation which the Convention voluntarily imposed on itself when it adopted the report of the Commission of Cooperative Program last year.[6]

Following acceptance of the above report, the Convention appointed the Efficiency Committee to study the agencies of the Convention and report concerning the Education Board. The committee reported favorably to the Convention but with a divided vote. A counter motion was made by Dr. Charles E. Maddry of North Carolina to dissolve the Board. This resulted in the Convention appointing another committee to study the specific problems of the Education Board and report to the same Convention. The new committee reached no agreement and reported the next day that they could not find a solution.

Maddry then reintroduced his resolution. This time he made a five-point proposal that dissolved the Board and ordered all property and responsibilities transferred to the Executive Committee of the Convention "as early as may be practical."

The problem of accountability is reflected in the Board's own report to the 1928 Convention that during the eight-year period of 1919–1927 over $204,000 had been spent in promoting and improving Ridgecrest. During this same period, the mortgaged debt on the assembly was almost $377,000. The value of the assembly property was reported to the 1927 Convention to be in excess of

$700,000. The transfer of property to the Executive Committee was evaluated at only $605,416.84.

With the Education Board's transfer of all responsibility for the assembly to the Executive Committee, the second era of the Southern Baptist Assembly at Ridgecrest closed.

---

[1] *Southern Baptist Convention Annual,* 1920, 524.
[2] *Southern Baptist Convention Annual,* 1923, 31.
[3] *Southern Baptist Convention Annual,* 1924, 31.
[4] *Southern Baptist Convention Annual,* 1925, 432.
[5] *Southern Baptist Convention Annual,* 1926, 48.
[6] *Southern Baptist Convention Annual,* 1927, 92.

Blue Mont (Terrell), North Carolina, about 1910

Front porch of Tucker cabin, where Spilman led the first worship service at Ridgecrest.

The first Pritchell Inn was opened officially August 1, 1914.
It had 54 bedrooms, a dining room, and a kitchen.

Pritchell Hall after remodeling in 1926. The dual front porches were
replaced by large colonial columns.

Old Pritchell Hall was removed in 1962. Present Pritchell Hall was opened in 1964.

First auditorium while still under construction

Fox Auditorium was completed in 1909 and was used until it was destroyed by wind March 1, 1914. This photo shows some of the 1910 participants.

Spilman Auditorium, including a classroom facility at the rear, was built in 1938–39.

Spilman Auditorium was enlarged in 1953 by extending the front of the building, beginning between the fifth and sixth upper story windows.

The totally renovated and enlarged present Spilman Auditorium was completed in 1972. The new building incorporated the older structure into its design.

Southern Baptist Assembly about 1930

Stage Coach House, the site of the first gathering of stockholders to organize the Southern Baptist Assembly Corporation. Side room and porch are later additions.

Ridgecrest Baptist Assembly about 1952

Interior of Stage Coach House, now Ridgecrest Museum

Spilman Lodge, built in 1942 from logs cut on the campus, is thought to be the largest log building in the Southeast.

Early development of the Southern Baptist Assembly

8 Years of Transition

He that putteth his trust in me shall possess the land, and shall inherit my holy mountain (Isa. 57:13).

The Southern Baptist Assembly at Ridgecrest was deeply involved and vitally affected by the actions of the Education Board and the actions of the Southern Baptist Convention concerning the Board. Some even blamed the assembly for causing the problem. The assembly later was referred to as "a tremendous responsibility that bankrupted one Board."

Part of Maddry's resolution stated: "That the Executive Committee of this Convention be recognized as the successor in law to the Board of Education, and that all the interests and obligations of the Education Board, financial, legal and otherwise be and are hereby committed to the Executive Committee of the Convention."[1]

This brief statement passed to the Executive Committee two mammoth problems, neither of which it was prepared for or capable of handling. The financial transfer, of course, included all the debt that had accumulated as well as the assets. The second and most pressing problem was the summer program. The Executive Committee was not a program agency. It had neither the personnel for this task nor the allocated finances for the program.

The program remained primary. The Convention was willing to struggle with the financial problems because of the benefits of the program to the Convention. During the years the Education Board managed the assembly, program expenses and operational expenses had not always been separated or clearly defined. Spilman had insisted during his management that separate accounts be maintained and that each section clearly account for its own expenses.

The uncertainty created by the financial condition caused many to ask if the assembly should be sold. Spilman himself raised the question: "Will there be any tomorrow with such a debt hanging over the property of the Assembly?" He raised the question, however, as an introduction to a speech pleading for the continuation of the assembly as a vital part of Southern Baptist life. He based his plea primarily on the advantages received through the annual summer program.

Spilman reaffirmed his belief that the assembly should operate the program on a sound financial basis and that it could generate its own operating funds if relieved of a debt that neither legally nor ethically was the responsibility of the assembly. Spilman recalled that the assembly was financially sound when it was transferred to the Education Board. He remarked: "The stockholders and their friends bought the land at Ridgecrest and developed it to the value represented when it was transferred to the Southern Baptist Convention. It was a well-established institution, practically free from debt, with subscriptions enough easily to clear all of the debt and put the assembly on its feet. It was taking care of its operation without drawing on any denominational treasury for a cent."[2]

Spilman fully believed and publically affirmed that the assembly could operate on a sound financial basis as it had in the past. He challenged the Executive Committee to accept this position, stating: "I make this most earnest plea to the Executive Committee of the Southern Baptist Convention not to sacrifice this splendid kingdom asset here on this mountain top upon the altar of the god of grumbling discontent in order that we may save a few dollars to keep in our pockets or to spend for the things which perish with the using. Pool this debt with all of our other obligations; give assurance that the work at Ridgecrest shall be permanent. We can operate the summer program without calling on the cooperative treasury for funds."[3]

Unsettled financial conditions had a depressing effect on the assembly's programming through the years. The uncertainty of year-to-year financing kept long-range program plans from developing. For example, the school of theology struggled from year to year, never knowing whether it would exist the next summer. The school met every year after its 1916 beginning, but always under a cloud and never really reaching its potential. In spite of an outstanding faculty each year, attendance usually was low. Advertising could not be done on a long-range basis. By the time the school was announced for each summer, many students already had chosen other similar educational programs.

The Executive Committee recognized that it was not equipped to handle the enormous task of program planning, faculty enlistment, advertising, and program conducting that the assembly required. Once again, the assembly turned to the resources of the Sunday School Board. By March 1929, a temporary working agreement had been completed. The Executive Committee happily reported to the 1929 Convention: "An agreement has been made with the Baptist Sunday School Board to operate the Southern Baptist Assembly, Ridgecrest, North Carolina, for a period of three years and that, too, without expense to the Executive Committee."[4]

Dr. I. J. Van Ness, executive secretary of the Board, was led to accept the responsibilities of Ridgecrest as a strategic challenge. He wanted the Board to be sure that it exercised the most prudent stewardship possible over the three-year period.

The original agreement with the Executive Committee did not place the responsibility for maintenance on the Sunday School Board. R. F. Staples, employed by the Education Board in 1925, remained with the assembly and was responsible to the Executive Committee for the maintenance of the property. Funds, however, simply were not available for adequate care of the facility.

Van Ness realized that maintenance problems had to be cared for or programs would suffer and guests would not continue to use the facility. He also recognized that problems would increase unless the buildings were adequately maintained. Under the direction of the Sunday School Board, the assembly continued to be available to every agency of the Convention for their programs.

In September 1929, Van Ness asked the Sunday School Board to commit itself to maintaining the assembly facility and to putting it on a sound financial basis. Van Ness stated:

> I wish to recommend that the Sunday School Board say to the Executive Committee that the condition of the

property and the charges connected with its management will require all the revenue in sight for this and the succeeding year. . . . There are some improvements which will be made if the property is to be available for an advance program. . . . The most important, however, are: that the buildings shall be painted. They ought not to go another winter. As there was a margin of funds left over, I ventured to tell the manager of the property to proceed at once before the bad weather comes on to repaint the buildings, deeming this, as I stated, necessary to their preservation. . . . It is my conviction that the Sunday School Board, having entered upon this enterprise, should endeavor at the end of the three years to turn the property back on a paying basis, if at all possible. This will require all revenues from this year and from next, which later must be anticipated."[5]

Following the successful summer of 1930, but still faced with continuing operational losses, the Board had to begin evaluating its agreement with the Executive Committee. The Board was able to handle the program costs and even the required expenses for property maintenance. It could not, however, assume or reduce the debt. The debt problems remained central as reflected in Van Ness's report to the Board.

His report read: "The hotel does not furnish sufficient facilities to make an adequate income to do more than balance the accounts. . . . Under these circumstances, as had been recited, I do not feel that the Board should make any definite commitments on the Ridgecrest management beyond next summer. . . pending the time when readjustment of the indebtedness can be made so that Ridgecrest shall bear only its own proper proportion of this indebtedness and be able to dispose of property to individuals with some assurance of permanence."[6]

Van Ness and Spilman shared the view that the assembly could operate if the debt was removed. Van Ness, in that statement, recognized that the assembly probably could handle its legitimate portion of the debt. The mortgage on Ridgecrest created by money spent on other Convention institutions needed to be identified and cared for by other means. Neither Spilman nor Van Ness ever asked that legitimate debts created by money spent on the assembly be paid by any entity other than the assembly.

With the three-year agreement about to expire, the Executive Committee had no resources for programming and maintaining the assembly. The committee, therefore, requested that the 1932 Convention approve the sale of the assembly to the Sunday School Board at a purchase price of $204,366.84. This figure represented the value of the assets at that time. The Executive Committee would pay the difference between the selling price and the bonded indebtedness.

Some funds were needed immediately to pay obligations due. The Executive Committee proposed that the Board pay a pro rata share of the interest and principle due on the bonds. Shares would be based on the $204,366.84 selling price and the current $281,000 value of outstanding bonds. The committee also requested the Board to make two payments of $4,563.12 each on the water system. All the advanced funds paid by the Board would be deducted from the original selling price.

The Sunday School Board did not feel it could accept the large debt. It was willing to extend the three-year agreement for programming and maintenance while a study of the matter was conducted. The Board formally replied in June as follows:

> Recognizing the seriousness of the financial emergency now upon Southern Baptist and feeling a deep sense of denominational responsibility for all our obligations, financial as well as moral and social, yet at the same time being deeply conscious of our responsibilities to the whole denomination for maintaining the financial integrity of the Sunday School Board and safeguarding its appointed program in our Baptist life, we, the members of the Sunday School Board, feel:
> 1. That we cannot accept the proposition presented to us by the Executive Committee whereby the property at Ridgecrest would be transferred to us;
> 2. That a committee should be appointed to work with the executive secretary of our Board, keeping the

problem of Ridgecrest under advisement, and to confer with the Executive Committee of the Southern Baptist Convention with a view to aiding them in devising a feasible plan for handling the emergency now upon them as a result of the debt on Ridgecrest, any action by the two to be reported to the next Southern Baptist Convention as per the instructions of the Convention at St. Petersburg.[7]

The Sunday School Board continued to accept more and more responsibility for the operation of Ridgecrest. In 1934, the original charter was dissolved. In 1935, the Sunday School Board requested that the official name be changed from the Southern Baptist Assembly to Ridgecrest Baptist Assembly.

Two significant personnel changes were made in 1935. R. F. Staples resigned after 10 years of service under the most difficult circumstances. As mentioned earlier, frequent changes of business managers was a problem in the early days. Staple's longer tenure added stability at a time when continuity was essential. Even though his tenure was plagued by constant lack of funds and uncertainty, he accomplished an amazing amount of development with very limited funds. He was replaced by Perry Morgan. Staple's philosophy of stewardship is reflected in an advertising brochure for the last season of his administration. The brochure closed with these words: "We are offering these rates for the coming year fully aware that prices are advancing, hoping that we may be able to break even, at least. We are doing this in order to give the conference full benefit of the doubt and to help our people come to Ridgecrest at the lowest possible cost."[8]

That same year Dr. T. L. Holcomb was elected executive secretary-treasurer of the Sunday School Board, replacing Van Ness. Holcomb carried the same appreciation for the Convention's need for Ridgecrest as Van Ness. In fact, Holcomb moved rapidly to help strengthen the operation. He felt that a long-range plan must be made for the development and operation of the assembly.

Holcomb appointed a committee from the Board to work with a special committee from the Executive Committee to work out a long-range agreement. The Executive Committee reported to the

1935 Convention that the Board had agreed to operate the assembly through the summer of 1940. This agreement continued to be successful and acceptable. The arrangement would provide a program each summer and "keep up" the property. The hotels were overflowing; dining and auditorium capacities were overtaxed. A turnaround had occurred. Multitudes were streaming to the mountain.

Faith led Ridgecrest through discouragement, hardship, financial crises, and other barriers, including vocal critics who wanted to rid the Convention of the assembly and its problems. All of these factors worked together to strengthen the faith of men all across the denomination. The words of James 1:3, "Knowing this, that the trying of your faith worketh patience," were experienced over and over again. At times it seemed that patience was taxed to its limits. Faith and patience, however, won the battle; and success was celebrated atop the "mountain of faith."

---

[1] *Southern Baptist Convention Annual,* 1927, 55.
[2] President's Address, 1928.
[3] Ibid.
[4] *Southern Baptist Convention Annual,* 1929, 65.
[5] Minutes of the Sunday School Board Meeting, September 1929.
[6] Minutes, October 1930.
[7] Minutes, June 1932.
[8] Advertising brochure issued by the Education Board (undated).

9 Faith Vindicated

Commit thy way unto the LORD; trust also in him; and he shall bring it to pass (Ps. 37:5).

The Sunday School Board's relationship with the assembly could be described by many expressions. Perhaps one of the best would be that of a father overseeing the growth of a child. Ridgecrest was born with the Board as its institutional parent. Spilman was able to spend time and money at Ridgecrest from the Board's resources, and that allowed Ridgecrest to come into being. The fatherly contributions of the Board were felt at every point in the history of the assembly.

The influence of the Sunday School Board in the operation of Ridgecrest continued to grow. The Board was not a rescue squad, appearing only briefly to meet an emergency need. It was a father who extended a hand to lift a stumbling child many times. As the child neared adulthood, the Board and the assembly became partners, much like a father takes his son into the business as an associate.

The partnership agreement, which began in 1929 and extended into 1940, exemplified the Board's stewardship of and devotion to the assembly. The Board continued to spend large amounts of money to keep the property in good condition and the program growing, all as a contribution to the assembly and to the Convention.

Holcomb and the Executive Committee expressed their satisfaction with the working arrangements and their desire for long-range planning by extending the agreement several years before it expired. In December 1937, they met to discuss needed improvements and future needs beyond the 1940 date. An agreement was reached that extended the Board's operation of the assembly through December 1950. This new agreement opened the door for expansion through building new permanent facilities.

The Executive Committee specifically asked the Board to build an auditorium adequate for the large crowds attending the assembly. The committee also requested that ample classrooms be provided as a part of the new unit. The old auditorium in Rhododendron Hall was to be remodeled into bedrooms, and additional dining room facilities were to be provided. The Board agreed to provide all these improvements for an amount not to exceed $60,000.

The Board invested these funds and all maintenance funds in the assembly with the understanding that the funds would not be repaid if the agreement were not extended beyond 1950. Provision was made that, in the event Ridgecrest was sold, the Board would be reimbursed for all capital expenditures.

In 1938–1939, a new auditorium was completed and named for the man who gave so much to the founding of Ridgecrest. The B. W. Spilman Auditorium memorialized "a dream come true."[1] The auditorium has been remodeled and enlarged twice, and it stands today with the original structure as the core and cornerstone of the present facility. Additional classrooms were added as an annex in 1948.

A new hotel was built behind Pritchell Hall in 1942. Each of its 30 rooms included a private bath. The modern structure was erected at a cost of approximately $15,000.

A highlight of this period came that same year. The Southern Baptist Convention gradually had reduced its debt load. It was able to consolidate all of the indebtedness of Convention agencies into one loan. The Convention secured funds from the First National Bank of New York City and removed the mortgage from the Ridgecrest property. This opened the door for the Sunday School Board to reconsider the previous offer of ownership.

In 1943, the Convention paid off all of its debts through the "one hundred thousand club" under the leadership of Dr. James E. Dillard. The slogan "debt free in '43" was realized, setting the stage for Ridgecrest to enter a new era.

In 1944, the Southern Baptist Convention formally approved the transfer of Ridgecrest Baptist Assembly from the Executive Committee to the Sunday School Board. The recommendation presented to the Convention reads as follows:
We therefore recommend:

1. That the Convention authorize and instruct the Executive Committee of the Southern Baptist Convention to transfer to the Sunday School Board of the Southern Baptist Convention by deed the property it holds at Ridgecrest, North Carolina, known as the Southern Baptist Assembly, to be held in trust for the Convention just as the property is now held by the Executive Committee. The Sunday School Board is to assume all obligations implicit in this ownership.

2. That it is the will and the instruction of the Convention that the Ridgecrest property be operated as the Southern Baptist Assembly, representing all phases of the Southern Baptist Convention work, and that all agencies of the Convention cooperate with the Sunday School Board to this end.

3. That a central section of the property to be agreed upon by the Executive Committee and the Sunday School Board shall be designated as the Assembly proper. Property within this zone, whether now owned by the Executive Committee or by the Sunday School Board, or property to be subsequently acquired, may not be sold without the action of the Southern Baptist Convention or its Executive Committee.

4. That major improvements on the property shall be provided for in agreement by and between the Executive Committee and the Sunday School Board.

5. That the details necessary for completing this transfer shall be worked out jointly by the Executive Committee and the Sunday School Board, and reported to the Convention.[2]

The Sunday School Board had some concern about this transfer of ownership of the Ridgecrest property. Every previous group that had held ownership to the assembly had experienced serious financial pressure created by Ridgecrest's operation.

Holcomb commented years later that the next meeting of the Sunday School Board following the 1944 Convention was one of the saddest the Board ever held. The Board members realized they had been given a tremendous responsibility that had played a significant role in the dissolving of one Board. They also could remember the great amount of money required by the Sunday School Board just to operate the facility for another owner.

The faith that had carried the assembly through so many clouds would express itself again through men dedicated to the Lord. Their willingness to accept the responsibility placed on them seems best described in a statement attributed to one Board member at the "saddest" meeting. "Well, they have given us their liability. Let's take it and make it into a denominational asset." And they did.

The agreements requested by the Convention were worked out over the next year. A special committee assigned to the task met at Ridgecrest August 9, 1944. Agreements were drafted that reflected the will of the Convention as expressed in the previous recommendations. The actual transfer of the property was completed September 5, 1944. The committee reported to the 1945 Convention the results of its work.

Several parts of that agreement are significant. First, the Sunday School Board as legal owner was to hold the assembly in trust for all the Convention. This was not necessarily because of Spilman, but it reflected his dream and purpose for the assembly.

Second, safeguards were included to prevent the Sunday School Board from making the same mistakes made by the Education Board. New buildings required joint approval of the Board and the Executive Committee. This was to prevent excessive building that might create financial obligations the Executive Committee would be forced to absorb.

Third, the agreement defined a core area that Ridgecrest would endeavor to develop. The Board also agreed to buy back property that had been sold to private individuals, churches, or other denominational agencies through the years. Due to the vast amount of private property, some highly developed, this did not prove feasible. The original circumference of the property was reduced many years later. A few small parcels within the smaller perimeter still remain under private ownership.

At the Board of Directors meeting in August 1928, following the Convention's action to dissolve the Education Board, Spilman predicted: "If the Executive Committee of the Southern Baptist Convention gives encouragement to this movement we shall have here on this mountain top in 20 more years an Assembly ground of which every Baptist in all the land will be justly thankful to God."[3]

The Executive Committee gave that encouragement and attention through the Sunday School Board. The committee moved on a schedule that exceeded Spilman's expectations. The transfer of property to the Sunday School Board in 1944 only finalized the growth in that direction that had taken place in cooperation with the Executive Committee.

Ridgecrest's mountain of faith stood tall, calling people from across the nation to sample its beauty, refreshing air, and God-inspired educational experiences.

---

[1] These words became the theme for several writers about the time of the 50th anniversary. R. L. Middleton also used these words as the title for his history of Ridgecrest.

[2] *Southern Baptist Convention Annual,* 1944, 33–34.

[3] President's Address, 1928.

10 Beyond the Dream

Enlarge the place of thy tent, and let them stretch forth the curtains of thine habitations: spare not, lengthen thy cords, and strengthen thy stakes (Isa. 54:2).

The prophet Isaiah's words followed a time of hardship and disappointment in Israel, but his words of encouragement sounded a new note to the nation. Brighter days were ahead. The time of growth and expansion had arrived. Isaiah's words could have been shouted from the top of the mountain as a new era opened for Ridgecrest. A new day had dawned.

The Sunday School Board moved quickly to meet some of the pressing needs for Ridgecrest. However, the opening days of that era were not without problems. The normal pains of transition were aggravated by the illness of business manager Perry Morgan. Morgan had served eight years from 1936 to 1944; but beginning in early 1943, he faced serious illness. Dr. J. N. Barnette of the Sunday School Department of the Sunday School Board agreed to serve as acting manager for the summer of 1943. He also served for the summer of 1944. Morgan resigned in December 1944 because of ill health.

By 1945, World War II had raged four years. The country was experiencing shortages in many areas. J. N. Barnette later recalled stories of his adventures in procuring food. He said that at times he had to buy sugar from the North Carolina bootleggers, since that was the only available source. Labor was in extremely short supply. Travel was restricted by federal order.

In the spring of 1945, representatives of the Sunday School Board met with officials of the Transportation Department in

Washington. The Board representatives agreed that their first priority was to cooperate with the nation's citizens. The program for the summer of 1945 was canceled. For the first time since the summer of 1909 no program was conducted at Ridgecrest.

The Sunday School Board used this time to search for a new manager to replace Perry Morgan. Ridgecrest's growing ministry called for a man with a wide range of skills. After a diligent search, the Board selected Robert Guy, who had gained administrative experience with the Baptist Hospital of Atlanta, Georgia, and Moore General Hospital, a veteran's hospital near Ridgecrest.

Guy was delayed in coming because of extended military service. The Board again asked J. N. Barnette to serve as acting manager for the summer of 1946. Perhaps the delay was providential. Guy later recalled: "Mr. Barnette, who came here [to Ridgecrest] during the summer, ran the assembly under the most adverse circumstances that you could imagine. . . . Food was hard to get. Sugar and meat were rationed. I have thought many times that had I come during that summer, I just do not believe I would have stayed; [but] the Lord has a way of working these things out."[1]

The Sunday School Board felt that conditions had stabilized enough for efforts to be made toward expanding the facilities to meet the needs of the anticipated attendance. Plans designed earlier for a new dining hall were approved, and funds were appropriated at the December Board meeting. By March 1947, a construction contract had been awarded.

The combination dining hall and classroom building was built of concrete and brick, and set the stage for changing from wooden structures at the assembly. The dining hall was spacious and attractive. The first floor dining hall increased the dining capacity to over 2,000 people per meal. The second floor classroom was a welcome addition to the limited auditorium classroom space. The enlarged dining area required larger kitchen facilities, which were added in 1948. The first paved streets were completed during the summer of 1947.

Attendance continued to grow, and by the close of the decade over 20,000 people could be expected to attend the annual sessions. The 1950 season registered approximately 22,000 guests. In

October of that year, Guy resigned to return to hospital administration.

The Sunday School Board took only one month to choose a successor to Guy. In November 1950, Willard K. Weeks became the manager. He, like Guy, may have felt that a delay in coming was providential. The Board had requested in 1946 that he accept the position, but he did not feel led to accept the invitation. By the time the invitation was renewed in 1950, he felt the Lord was directing him into assembly ministry.

Weeks was born about the time Spilman began to dream about Ridgecrest. The year Spilman died, Weeks assumed responsibility for the assembly. He was the first man to manage the assembly affairs longer than Spilman. On his first trip to Ridgecrest in 1937, Weeks invested some money in Ridgecrest. Perry Morgan sold him one of the lots set aside for private cottages. In 1950, Weeks returned to invest his life in the conference center. The 17 years of Weeks' administration were marked by steady, well-planned expansion that carried the assembly beyond the dreams of its founders.

In 1950–1951, another multipurpose building was added in the middle of the assembly grounds. The new building was appropriately named the Center Building. Through the years, the building has lived up to its name; not only by location, but also by serving as the center of attraction for guests. The building, designed to complement the landscape, looks like three separate buildings. The lower floor opens to the east and originally contained a beauty shop, a barber shop, an office for the Relief and Annuity Board (Annuity Board), and a storage area.

The second story opened to the south facing Pritchell Hall and contained the Baptist Book Store. The third floor opened to the west and housed the always-popular Nibble Nook. The outstanding feature, among many refreshment items at the Nibble Nook, was the Ridgecrest ice cream cone. Over 40 years later, the hand-dipped cone is still a major attraction. The total cost of this spacious three-story building was less than $60,000.

A major concern of this period was the water supply. Water, which seemed so abundant as the original group toured the grounds, had gradually diminished. The vast number of people attending the conference center had increased the demand for water beyond the capacity of the system built in late 1927 and early 1928. Weeks later recalled, "I know that we pumped continuously night and day in order to get enough water to even do the minor things that were necessary."[2]

A large parcel of land on the back of the campus, later known as the Belk Property, was essential to the expansion of the water system. The property lay between Ridgecrest and Montreat conference centers and was owned by the Presbyterians. Mr. Belk was a Presbyterian and wanted to continue to hold the property as a buffer zone for his Presbyterian friends at Montreat.

Willard Weeks recalled making about 12 trips to Charlotte to talk to Belk about letting Ridgecrest purchase the land. Working with their real estate agent, the Ridgecrest negotiators felt they were about ready to close the sale when Belk died. This delayed the sale closing until after Belk's will was probated and the estate was settled. Finally, in 1953 the call came informing Weeks that the Belk heirs had agreed to complete the sale.

However, the delay was profitable for the assembly. The family also wanted to honor a pledge Belk had made to Davidson College. In order to raise the needed cash, the heirs offered the land to Ridgecrest for $25,000. The Board made a counter offer of $18,750, which was readily accepted. That may be the most vital property investment the Board ever made at Ridgecrest. The conference center's growth over the next few years, and Ridgecrest today, could not have occurred without the water supply the Belk property provided.

Ridgecrest leaders hoped the watershed would produce enough water to fill a one-million-gallon earthen reservoir. When actual surveys were made and the best site selected, the projections far exceeded their hopes. When the dam was completed, the reservoir held over 10 million gallons. The cost of the project was only $39,000. A water supply that met the needs of the assembly until the late 1970s was complete with land and construction costing less than $60,000. An auxiliary concrete reservoir for storage of chlorinated water was added in 1955.

With this abundant supply of water, Weeks was able to expand the water system greatly. He laid over six and one-half miles of water pipes through the greater assembly area. He foresaw the need to conserve water, even if it appeared to be unlimited. As a conservation measure, he installed water meters so that charges to private users could be based on consumption rather than on a flat rate.

Another major 1952 project was the enlargement of Spilman Auditorium, which had been built in 1938–1939. Attendance had grown to exceed the auditorium's capacity. The front of the building was extended with a new porch, and colonial columns were added. This "new" auditorium had a seating capacity of 3,500, including the balcony and the open classrooms located on each side and at the rear.

T. L. Holcomb retired from the Sunday School Board in 1953. Dr. James L. Sullivan was elected as the Board's new executive secretary. Like his predecessors, Sullivan felt that Ridgecrest was a vital part of Southern Baptist life. Because of the conference center's importance to the ministry of the Board and Southern Baptists, he was willing to continue to allocate as many resources as possible to meet all of the assembly's needs.

One of the first projects the Board considered was a building designed especially for children. The Education Division of the Board spent nearly two years studying the needs of younger children and determining the use of such a building. Construction began in 1955, and the building was in usable condition for the 1956 summer season. The building served as a center for teaching and training children. It also included specially designed observation booths for workers with children. Through the one-way screening, these workers could view trained workers in actual teaching sessions. Because of changes in age-grading, this unit is now the Preschool Building.

The first apartment complex was built in 1954 with eight efficiency units for families of six or less. Because of the popularity of the Florida Cove apartments, the building's roof was raised and a second floor was added in 1960, providing eight more units.

Nineteen fifty-seven was a jubilee year as Ridgecrest celebrated its 50th anniversary. The year was marked by several notable events, including dedication of the Children's Building. A special service that included a historical review, a dedication, and future planning was conducted in Spilman Auditorium July 24, 1957.

The anniversary year also was highlighted by the purchase of the Old Stage Coach House and property. This is the same property that was used for the called meeting to create the Southern Baptist Assembly Corporation in 1905. The Education Board had mortgaged the land and the Stage Coach Building. When the mortgage was not paid on time, ownership of the property was forfeited. The Sunday School Board and Ridgecrest were delighted to climax several years of trying to recover the property with the jubilee purchase. The Stage Coach Building was converted into a museum of Ridgecrest history and was a focal point of the celebrations.

The first 50 years saw many dreams fulfilled. All that Spilman had hoped for and more had come to pass. A great assembly "second to none" spread across the mountain. "Thousands swarmed" the beautiful acres. The assembly belonged to "the Baptist folk." Most important of all, the programs provided the educational experience necessary to strengthen the churches all across the Convention.

Fifty years of dedicated service of hundreds of individuals, faithful stewardship of several institutions, and the faith of multiplied thousands of Southern Baptists made Ridgecrest "a mountain of faith."

---

[1] In 1968 a group of people formerly connected with Ridgecrest were invited to a two day meeting to reminisce and record Ridgecrest history as they remembered it. The conference was recorded and later transcribed, but remains unpublished.

[2] Ibid.

11 A Developing Mountain

They that wait upon the LORD shall renew their strength; they shall mount up with wings as eagles; they shall run, and not be weary; and they shall walk, and not faint (Isa. 40:31).

The second 50 years opened with the most successful season in the history of Ridgecrest. The official registration showed 31,980 in attendance at the summer sessions. This exceeded the jubilee year by 743 guests. Training Union (now Discipleship Training) led in attendance with 3,678 registered for the third week. The first and second weeks registered 3,236 and 3,465 respectively.

The Sunday School Board continued to expand the assembly by building new hotels, apartments, and additional classroom space. As facilities were added, attendance continued to grow. It is always easy to write history in terms of buildings built and assets acquired. However, neither buildings nor attendance figures record Ridgecrest's greatest contribution. The program was always foremost in the eyes of those who developed the assembly.

T. L. Holcomb stated the principal clearly when he reported to the Sunday School Board members in December 1937. He reminded them to keep "first things first. Spiritual things are given first place at Ridgecrest. Whatever else we do, our aim is first of all to minister to the spiritual life of those who come to the Assembly. Our desire and aim is to create and maintain an atmosphere in which a Christian can grow in soul and spirit, and be more useful in Kingdom work. An effort is made, of course, to minster to the recreational and social side of life and provide physical comforts for all who come to the conferences; but these are not foremost in our efforts to make the Assembly a spiritual force from the top of these great hills of God to the uttermost parts of the earth."[1]

Unfortunately records are not available on the number of Southern Baptists who, through the years, made life-changing commitments at Ridgecrest. The apostle Paul reminded the Corinthian church: "While we look not at the things which are seen, but at the things which are not seen: for the things which are seen are temporal; but the things which are not seen are eternal" (2 Cor. 4:18).

The mountain air, the beauty of the landscape, the majestic buildings, and the mountain itself all blended with the teaching and training faculty to make Ridgecrest a spiritual gathering point for Southern Baptists. Because of what happened to people, the Sunday School Board continued to help with expansion and improvement. Much has been written concerning what the Sunday School Board and others contributed to the assembly, contributions reflected in building and maintenance budgets. Perhaps greater amounts were invested in programming costs. No fees were changed to recover these costs.

The practice of not charging for the program beyond freewill offerings was established in the assembly's beginning. A brochure, designed in 1911 for the purpose of raising endowment funds, answered the question, Why endow Ridgecrest? "Because of its purpose. It [Ridgecrest] was not established as a money-making institution, nor is it primarily a health resort. No admission fee is charged to the grounds, nor is any fee charged for any of the services in the auditorium."[2]

The brochure further stated that "the Ridgecrest Assembly has as one of its primary purposes the giving of a wider vision of the affairs of the kingdom. An admission fee charged at the gates would bar many from the benefits of the Assembly, often those who stand most in need of its benefits."[3] The official program for the summer of 1910 showed that free admission did contain several restrictions (see chapter 6).

Through the years, charges had to be made for special programs, such as charges for the school of theology in order to pay the faculty. However, the spirit of offering the program without charge has been maintained with free access to all for the worship experiences and most other activities.

The Sunday School Board developed a policy of charging for room, board, and other services. The program costs were borne by the organization conducting the program. The large number of enlisted faculty required, the number of employees involved, and the travel and honorarium expenses all add up to a considerable expense for each week's program.

In 1960, the Sunday School Board adopted a formal statement setting forth the policy of recovering "all costs of food service, room service, recreation, camps and farms and garden expenses from guests." The cost of "space used for meetings, exhibits, programs, agency offices, book stores, gift shop, Nibble Nook, and so forth was to be recovered from charges made to the programs and organizational units using [the facilities]." The statement was included as a part of the *Objectives for the Program of Assembly Operations*.

This policy has been amended many times through the years. However, the basic concept still is in operation. The organizations sponsoring the programs in the summer season bear the cost of the programs. Through the years, agencies and departments continue to feel that this is one of the best investments they make in reaching Southern Baptists with programs and ministries.

Building projects of various sizes were completed each year. While it would not be practical to mention each one, several deserve special recognition.

By 1962, those "temporal things seen" had served their usefulness. The time had come for some of the major landmarks to be replaced. Such a time always arrives with mixed emotions. The desire to maintain the past contrasts with the longing to look to the future. Stately Pritchell Hall symbolized all the trials and tribulations of those early days. A masterpiece of construction at its birth in 1914, Pritchell stood for 48 years, serving Southern Baptists from all across the land.

Pritchell was remodeled and "modernized" in 1925–1926 and was given its stately appearance with the addition of the white colonial columns. This hallmark of Ridgecrest, a tribute to the days gone by, stood in the center of the campus. It, too, had to pass to make room for tomorrow.

At the close of the 1962 season, "Old Pritchell" was torn down to make room for a new multipurpose building. The "New Pritchell" stands today as the centerpiece of the campus. It serves as the registration area, usually the first point of service for thousands of conference center guests. The building contains the administrative offices, over 200 hotel rooms, a first aid area, two large guest lobbies, the gift shop, a press office, and multiple other services for guests. New Pritchell was opened for guests in the summer of 1964 with a special dedication service held July 29.

The new Pritchell Hall opened a new era for Ridgecrest. Expansion had been rapid and continuous. The time had come for assets to be channeled more toward replacement, remodeling, and keeping Ridgecrest as modern as the rest of the educational world. This had to be done without compromising the spiritual values of Ridgecrest and without losing sight of its primary purpose as an educational facility for the masses.

Another landmark was replaced following the 1965 season. Rhododendron Hall, built in 1925–1926, was removed to make room for a new concept in Ridgecrest growth. Rhododendron's replacement was completely winterized. This made the use of Ridgecrest during winter possible for the first time.

The new Rhododendron Hall was more than a building replacement. The hall was a unique building, designed in part with the Foreign Mission Board to allow them to expand their missionary training program. The Sunday School Board and Foreign Mission Board worked out a two-year agreement for use of the facility. The building was designed to provide bedrooms, kitchen and dining facilities, conference rooms, offices, and lounge areas for the new missionary orientation program. This allowed the Foreign Mission Board to provide each missionary with 16 weeks of intensive training before leaving for a chosen field of service.

The new Rhododendron Hall was completed by September 1967, and the first missionary orientation session was held that fall. The orientation program was extremely beneficial to the Foreign Mission Board and still is carried on today at other locations. The assembly also had full use of the mission orientation facility for summer programs.

Willard Weeks completed 17 years of service and retired October 1, 1967. The outward appearance of the assembly had changed completely and remarkably during his ministry at Ridgecrest. However, concern for meeting the needs of people and churches was still foremost. Kenneth McAnear was elected by the Sunday School Board to succeed Weeks as manager. He began his service August 16, 1967.

Before McAnear arrived, plans had been developed for a 64-room hotel to be erected behind Rhododendron Hall. The Sunday School Board let the contract for this building in the summer of 1967. When construction, including a covered walk to Rhododendron and the dining hall building, was completed by the middle of the 1968 season, housing capacity for the Foreign Mission Board's orientation more than doubled.

That same year construction on 32 Royal Gorge apartments began. These apartments were erected in the 1969 season for use by the assembly maintenance staff. Like all recent construction, they replaced older housing units. The individual rustic cottages built in the early days were gradually disappearing.

During the 1969 calendar year, the assembly began to make limited facilities available to churches for weekend retreats and special small conferences. This small start was the beginning of a whole new era of programming. The beginning was shaky due to the newness of the idea. The program was hampered by limited facilities, limited winter service personnel, and lack of promotion; but it was a beginning—a beginning of what was to become a productive part of the assembly's program in just a few years.

In February 1971, the Sunday School Board created a new division of work dealing exclusively with Ridgecrest and Glorieta assemblies. The new arrangement provided for better long-range planning and development into new areas of service.

The winter program continued to be plagued by mass cancellations and "no-shows." The use of the facility by some non-Baptist groups raised legal questions concerning the tax position of the assembly as a nonprofit organization. The uncertainty led to several decisions and finally to a brief cancellation of the winter program in the winter of 1970–1971.

During the 1970–1972 period, a complete study of the assembly's operational procedures was conducted. The study evaluated growth patterns for the future and developed a total design of the campus for future building projects. One primary decision concerned how large the assembly should be allowed to grow. Land areas available, water supplies, growth of state assemblies, and quality of the programs available had to be considered.

An expansion of Spilman Auditorium was a major factor. Some remodeling was required. Expansion was highly desirable. The size of the auditorium would determine the amount of support facilities that would be built. One program change that had gradually evolved through the years was toward more classroom teaching activities and less convocations. This expansion and future programming techniques had to be considered.

The study resulted in several significant decisions:

First, the assembly would be limited to facilities accommodating up to 2,600 people in conferences. Housing and meals accommodations would be limited to 2,000. This plan would allow for 600 persons to be accommodated by private facilities that had been developed over the years.

Second, the winter program would be developed and made an integral part of the assembly's total operation. The assembly was given permission to program winter conferences. This excluded any area of programming specifically assigned to any other Convention agency or commission. The assembly would be responsible for winter sales to groups other than Southern Baptists and for programming conferences to utilize the facilities to the fullest.

Third, a long-range building plan was approved for erecting new units, remodeling present units, and removal of outdated units so the campus would meet the planning guidelines. A complete site plan, including the location of each new building, was approved. A color scheme was developed so that as each unit was repainted, it would blend into the color of the mountains and forest.

Fourth, in recognition of growth of the assembly and the new dimensions of its work, the Sunday School Board approved a change of name at the February 1972 meeting. The assembly was officially named Ridgecrest Baptist Conference Center.

The first stage of the building program concerned a new auditorium. After considerable study, the decision was made to enlarge, for the second time, Spilman Auditorium. However, this time a total renovation was planned. It literally became a new auditorium. In order to use the auditorium each summer, the project was divided into two parts. The first winter, the entire roof structure was replaced. The second winter, the entire interior was renovated with no time lost due to bad weather. All work could be done under the protection of the new roof. The new Spilman Auditorium was ready for use in 1972 and was dedicated July 30 of that year.

In February 1974, Dr. James L. Sullivan retired as president of the Sunday School Board, and Dr. Grady C. Cothen was elected president. Like his predecessors, Cothen continued to view the conference center as a major contributor to the success of the Sunday School Board's total ministry.

The winter program had grown significantly and had become a major influence in the conference center's operation. Cothen realized the winter months had the potential the Board needed to reach the churches with new methods at new times. He saw the need to allocate resources to improve programming opportunities.

The already-crowded summer program could not accommodate the additional requests for program time. Specialized ministries such as single adults, senior adults, families, young married persons, youth, and many others needed program time and a place to prepare them to fulfill their responsibilities.

Grady Cothen felt the conference centers could best meet these programming requests by offering a sound educational and attractively designed faculty to the agencies. In 1976, the Board created a Program and Promotion Section. This section's responsibility was to program and to enlist other agencies to program conferences during the winter months.

Through the new section's efforts, the conference center served 56,866 guests in 1980. The attendance was almost 60,000 in 1981.

In just a few short years, the conference center had come to serve almost as many guests in the winter as it served in the summer.

In 1977, construction of Interstate 40 began. Site planning for the new highway began in the mid 60s. When McAnear arrived at Ridgecrest in 1967, contractors were scheduled to begin work on Interstate 40 the next year. Over 10 years later, construction finally got under way and was completed in May 1980.

By the time the 1980s arrived, Ridgecrest was almost totally new. From the front gate, which had been redesigned to accommodate Interstate 40, to the back of the campus, which contained a new recreation park, everything looked new. Each conference room had been renovated, including carpet and air conditioning. Four air-conditioned hotels had been erected, and additional apartments had been built. Nearly every structure had been repainted in the new color scheme.

Fifteen assembly managers have served through the years to help bring the conference center to its current position of worldwide service. Each manager made some distinctive contribution. The managers and years of service are:

B. W. Spilman, General Manager/General Secretary . . 1907–1909
E. L. Hon 1910–1911
E. F. Mumford 1911–1913
C. E. Brewer 1913
Jesse Daniel Moore 1913–1915
B. W. Spilman, General Secretary 1916–1917
E. L. Hon, Acting Manager 1916–1917
H. B. Craven, Business Manager 1918–1920
Livingston Mays, Corresponding Secretary 1919–1922
Albert R. Bond, Corresponding Secretary 1922–1927
R. F. Staples 1925–1935
Perry Morgan 1936–1946
J. N. Barnette, Acting Manager 1945–1946
Robert Guy 1946–1950
Willard K. Weeks 1950–1967
Kenneth R. McAnear 1967–1992
G. W. Lankford 1992–Present

As we gaze on the beauty of Ridgecrest and recognize the accomplishments of these men, our minds go back to what Spilman saw that morning in 1906 when he stepped from the train to his first view of Ridgecrest. If Spilman walked across the assembly grounds today, his heart would be filled with joy and he would hear his Master say, "Well done, thou good and faithful servant" (Matt. 25:21).

Spilman gladly would share that commendation with all who worked with him and with all who served after him. The mountain belongs to God. Spilman claimed it for Him. Spilman planted; many watered; but God gave the increase. Gazing across the mountains, Spilman would recall how "faith wrought with his works, and by works was faith made perfect" (Jas. 2:22).

---

[1] Sunday School Board Minutes, December, 1937.
[2] From a brochure issued in 1911 to the stockholders to promote an endowment fund for Ridgecrest.
[3] Ibid.

12 Tomorrow: A New Day of Faith

Both riches and honour come of thee, and thou reignest over all; and in thine hand is power and might; and in thine hand it is to make great, and to give strength unto all (1 Chron. 29:12).

All of the first assembly grounds buildings have gone. In their place stand modern, efficient, convenient structures. For 75 years Southern Baptists have gone *up* to Ridgecrest. Like worshipers going to Jerusalem, we always go *up* to Ridgecrest All roads lead upward as we travel to the mountain of faith.

A young boy seated between the tall white columns of the first Pritchell Hall expressed the feelings of others: "Ridgecrest is a mountain where God is." The purpose of Ridgecrest is to be a place where men, women, boys, and girls gather to meet God in a special closeness of divine-human fellowship.

After a pause, the boy continued, "Yep, it is. God's right here, all right." Another replied, "He's down in the valleys, too." The boy said, "Sure, but He's nearer up here on the mountain."

The buildings have changed; the outward appearance is different; but people of faith meeting God in face-to-face encounters always will be the same. God's handiwork still is evident as worshipers strolls across the campus or off into the nearby woods. The assembly grounds now encompass over 2,000 acres of God-adorned, beautiful, quiet mountains. More than 600 varieties of flowering plants, wild fruits, and nuts are present in those mountains.

Sparkling springs and clear mountain streams sing God's praises as they flow unceasingly toward the oceans.

As marvelous as the physical assets of the assembly are, people always have been and always will be Ridgecrest's number one asset. All is in vain unless people find spiritual fulfillment on the mountain. If the buildings could speak, they would paraphrase the apostle Paul: "Though we stand as majestic as man can build and have not love, we will become as useless blocks of stone or rusting steel. Unless we help persons to use the gift of prophecy, to understand all mysteries, to gain all knowledge, to exercise all faith so that they can move mountains, and to abide in love, we are nothing" (1 Cor. 13:1-2).

Ridgecrest is more than land, buildings, and physical beauty. It is a sacred place—conceived in faith, built by faith, developed through the trials of faith, and committed to God by people of faith. But do we have faith for Ridgecrest's future?

B. W. Spilman wondered about the assembly's future as he faced the crucial question, Will there be a tomorrow? Twenty years had passed, and the future seemed dim. Many questioned the conference center's future during the difficult years of the Education Board's leadership. More than once, the option of selling the mountain was considered. But God's hand led through those times, and after 75 years Ridgecrest stands at the pinnacle of its strength.

The issue we face is not so much overcoming difficulty. The past has proven God's power again and again. Today the questions are: Can Ridgecrest live in its prosperity? Will its purpose be hidden behind the majestic buildings and the comforts they afford? Will people continue to seek first the kingdom of God and realize "the eternal values unseen"?

Ridgecrest must serve in the future as it has served in the past. The service to the Convention cannot be measured, but it must not be reduced. James L. Sullivan reminisced: "I don't know how in the world we would have ever built unity in our denomination without the Ridgecrest and Glorieta assemblies which are where North, South, East, and West come together to find a common denominator. It is well that they learn how much alike Baptists are."[1]

As it has been over the past 75 years, so may it be in the years ahead. May our focus be on unity, vision, wisdom, faith, and people. May dedicated men and women, serving in multitudes of positions, be our human strength; but may God's choosing, building, and using Ridgecrest for His will be our goal. For "Except the LORD build the house, they labour in vain that build it; except the LORD keep the city, the watchman waketh but in vain (Ps. 127:1).

---

[1] Sullivan in history recording session, 1968.

Appendix 1
Tributes

James H. Tucker

James H. Tucker is a man whose name should not be forgotten in the history of Ridgecrest. Tucker, superintendent of Sunday School, First Baptist Church, Asheville, North Carolina, and an eminent lawyer with a large and lucrative practice, gave his time and thought to the early days of Ridgecrest as no other person did.

Tucker selected the site for Ridgecrest and called it to the attention of the committee. He negotiated the multitude of details for securing options on the land (nine tracts) and closed the deals for all of it. He wrote all of the deeds and worked up the abstract of title to the property. Tucker wrote the charter and secured its adoption by the General Assembly of North Carolina. He introduced the resolution in the 1907 annual session of the Southern Baptist Convention meeting in Richmond, Virginia, to move forward with the development of Ridgecrest. James used his personal credit to secure funds for beginning the development of the property. He was Ridgecrest's first attorney, first chairman of the Board of Directors, and first chairman of the Executive Committee.

With untiring devotion, James H. Tucker gave himself to the work. His only financial compensation was four building lots on the assembly grounds. Without the help of this able, consecrated Christian lawyer, the accomplishments of the early days of Ridgecrest would have been impossible. He gave his time, legal ability, and money without reservation. In an address delivered to the annual meeting of the assembly stockholders, held in the assembly auditorium at Ridgecrest, Thursday, August 16, 1928, Tucker's comrade, B. W. Spilman, who stood by and helped as best he could in the early days of the assembly, paid rich tribute to his friend and helper.

Bernard Washington Spilman
The name B. W. Spilman and the phrase "faith that built a mountain" were synonymous. Tributes, histories, and biographies all reflect the influence of this man in the development of Ridgecrest. He lived to see his dream and vision fulfilled.

On January 1, 1941, B. W. Spilman retired from the Sunday School Board. His retirement closed his years of active service to Ridgecrest. By then, he was almost 70 years old. Well over half of his life had been invested in Ridgecrest. Spilman led the way from an idea to a recommendation and then to a beginning. He remained steadfast through good days and bad days and on to fulfillment of his dream. When others might have quit, he encouraged, prodded, and kept things moving.

Spilman often returned to the Ridgecrest campus as a visitor. He never lost his love for the assembly he founded. On Sunday, March 26, 1950, Bernard Washington Spilman died at his home in Kinston, North Carolina.

B. W. Spilman was a big man with a big heart. He allowed God to work through him as he envisioned a place where Christian leaders could go to receive training and spiritual renewal. Great faith was required to see beyond the many obstacles to the fulfillment of this dream. Spilman's deep faith and total commitment brought reality to his dream—the building of Ridgecrest, "mountain of faith."

Willard K. Weeks
Perhaps a man's true contributions can be measured best by those who follow in his footsteps. No one can appreciate Willard K. Weeks' service more than the one who followed him as manager of Ridgecrest Baptist Conference Center.

Weeks' contribution can only be summarized here. His ministry touched 18 years of Ridgecrest's life. From November 1950 to October 1967, he and his constant companion, Zelma, devoted full-time service to the assembly. With a stewardship of love and concern like that of B. W. Spilman, Weeks devoted all his energies to the assembly's development and operation.

Weeks served more years in actual management of the assembly than any other person. Literally thousands of summer staffers served under his leadership. Willard and Zelma, known as Pop and Mom, carried the assembly through hard years of institutional growth.

Perhaps one of Willard's finest contributions was the quality of employees he enlisted to carry out the assembly's ministry. The service of these people and Weeks' leadership have made my task much easier.

I am grateful to all who went before me, but my ministry has been affected most by Willard Weeks. Not only are Willard and Zelma my predecessors at the conference center, they also are my beloved friends in Christ.

——Kenneth McAnear

Appendix 2
Camp Ridgecrest for Boys and Camp Crestridge for Girls

A unique part of the Sunday School Board is the "camps ministry," operated as part of Ridgecrest Baptist Conference Center. Functionally, the camps are an integral part of the conference center. In terms of program, they are independent. Their programs are designed primarily for participants to remain four weeks. Actually, they may choose to stay any combination of weeks during a summer with a minimum of two weeks and a maximum of eight weeks.

The programs are designed for boys and girls between the ages of eight and sixteen. No chaperones or parents attend with the youth. A full range of faculty and staff are on hand to conduct the programs, provide food and lodging, serve as counselors, and provide personal supervision and guidance. The camps maintain a strong spiritual emphasis at all times. Young people's spiritual growth is the camps' primary goal.

Each camp has a rich history that demonstrates the camps' success. Scattered throughout the Southern Baptist Convention are thousands of staffers and campers who have achieved prominence in their chosen vocational fields. Men and women who have chosen church-related or other careers testify to the contributions to their lives of Camp Ridgecrest for Boys or Camp Crestridge for Girls.

The camps were not developed as a part of Spilman's activity or leadership. The present camps were started under the direction of the Sunday School Board and have remained a part of its ministry through the years.

An effort had been made to establish camps during the years of the Education Board's ownership. In 1924, a tract of land presently used by Camp Ridgecrest for Boys, was acquired. Considerable funds were invested in the development of the area. A major expenditure was the construction of the lake, located approximately in the center of the camp, and the purchase of a large house built by B. W. Spilman for his personal use. The area was named Camp Swannanoa.

A girl's camp was operated during the 1926 and 1927 seasons under the name "Camp Star Note." Mrs. J. M. Dawson of Waco, Texas, was camp director for both seasons.

When the Convention acted to transfer the assembly property to the Executive Committee, the camps were discontinued. The land, the lake, and all of the buildings were included in the transfer of ownership to the Executive Committee.

Camp Ridgecrest for Boys

The Executive Committee requested that the Sunday School Board develop programs and operate the assembly for a three-year period from 1929 to 1931. Dr. Noble Van Ness was the executive secretary-treasurer of the Board at the time. He had been very active in Boy Scout work for years and had a deep concern for the spiritual welfare of boys. He immediately set out to find a way to develop programs for boys at the assembly.

Van Ness found the answer to this need by utilizing the facilities of Camp Swannanoa to open a camp for boys for the summer of 1929. He looked for an outstanding Christian leader to serve as director. Van Ness enlisted Frank E. Burkhalter to oversee the total operation. The camp was programmed for one two-week trial session. The results were so rewarding that planning for the 1930 season was begun immediately.

Van Ness knew the key to success was to have a highly-regarded, qualified director. He selected Charles W. Burts, a young student at Yale, who had five years of experience as a counselor and assistant director in other private camps. Charles worked with Van Ness to enlarge the 1930 season. Based on the success of the first two-week session, they planned for eight weeks of camp. Burts served as director each summer through 1938.

Attendance was small during the first years. Burts later estimated that between 40 and 50 boys attended each session. The program offered a variety of activities, and a strong Christian emphasis permeated every aspect of camp life. A worship service was held early each morning and each evening.

The Indian lore motif that traditionally has been the camp trademark began in the 1930 season. The Ridgecrest Redskins have continued to meet in council rings over the years. The Indian lore was used to help young boys grow strong of heart and strong of physique, while the Christian emphasis led them to new spiritual heights.

One historic feature of Camp Ridgecrest for Boys is the large log building in the center of the campus. It was completed in 1942 and houses the kitchen, two dining hall wings, and a gymnasium. The gym area has a huge fireplace at one end that allows the area to be used for convocations and devotions in the cool mountain evenings. The building is considered the largest log building in the Southeast.

Camp Ridgecrest usually operated for one six-week session. Burts cut the season back from eight to six weeks after the 1930 season. In 1950 Perry Morgan felt the time had come to enlarge the camp and to enlist a full-time director.

George W. Pickering, a student from Mississippi College, had joined the camp staff in 1947. Because of Pickering's experience and his leadership abilities, Morgan looked to him for the guidance needed to move the camp forward. The six years George Pickering served the camp more than validated Morgan's wisdom. Pickering expanded the program from one six-week session to two five-week sessions, a move that allowed additional campers to experience Camp Ridgecrest.

Some of the camp's years have been more difficult than others; but overall, the camp's history glows with success. Richard Johnson became camp manager in 1973, and the camp celebrated its 50th birthday in 1978. Under his leadership, the camp experienced some of its most successful seasons. Attendance increased each year with a new high reached in 1981.

The camp still operates and maintains its primary commitment to boys' spiritual development. Each activity is designed to help them grow toward being the kind of persons God intends them to be.

Through the years, the strength of the staff has been a major factor in the camp's success. Listing the multitude of persons who have served as staffers is not practical. They are represented by the directors who enlisted them and directed their work.

Directors of Camp Ridgecrest for Boys

Frank E. Burkhalter	1929
Charles W. Burts	1930–1938
John W. Hughston, Jr.	1939–1940
J. D. (Red) Franks, Jr.	1941
Darrell C. Richardson	1942
Richard C. Burts, Jr.	1943
J. W. Hill	1944
Perry Morgan, Manager and Director	1945
Chaplain Nat. H. Brittain	1946–1947
James R. Howlett	1948–1949
George W. Pickering	1950–1955
Harry McCall, Jr.	1956–1958
Wayne Chastain	1959–1963
Ken Bryant	1964–1965
Darrell Richardson	1966–1968
Monroe Ashley	1969–1973
Rick Johnson	1974–1984
Ron Springs	1985–Present

Camp Crestridge for Girls

As early as 1926 an attempt was made to establish a girls' camp under the Education Board's supervision. Camp Star Note, the girls' portion of Camp Swannanoa, only operated in the summer of 1926 and 1927. Other brief attempts at short summer sessions were made, but none were successful enough to continue the operation.

These efforts, however, were enough to keep alive the hope and desire that one day a camp for girls similar to Camp Ridgecrest for Boys would be a reality. In 1950, those dreams began to take the form of concrete actions to establish such a camp.

T. L. Holcomb, executive secretary of the Sunday School Board, received a $25 check designated for a girls' camp. Holcomb planted that seed money immediately, and growth began with the formation of a committee to study the matter and select a site. Holcomb led the Board to allocate $100,000 for 1953 and $50,000 for 1954 to begin the development of a girls' camp.

George Pickering, director of Camp Ridgecrest for Boys, strongly supported the effort for a girls' camp. Many of the programming concepts and administrative techniques, which he developed in the boys' camp, were shared with the girls' camp to make its beginning much easier. He suggested that the name of the boys' camp with the syllables reversed be used as a name for the girls' camp, and Camp Crestridge for Girls was born.

Groundbreaking ceremonies were conducted on August 4, 1954. Heavy rains in the area forced the ceremony indoors. James L. Sullivan, the new executive secretary of the Sunday School Board, broke ground in a bucket of dirt. Construction started the next month, with the camp opening for the summer of 1955.

As early as 1952, Willard Weeks, manager of Ridgecrest Baptist Assembly, began the search for a director for Camp Crestridge. The same high quality director and staff demanded at Ridgecrest were required for Crestridge. Pickering aided Weeks in the search and was the first to meet Miss Arvine Bell, the one who would direct the camp for almost 25 five years.

Arvine Bell was selected as the person who could make Camp Crestridge for Girls the camp everyone wanted. She began her work in 1954. She is the only full-time director to serve the camp. The camp, its development, staff, and the hundreds of young women across the Convention who have attended Crestridge all stand as testimonies to the effectiveness of her ministry.

Crestridge opened for its first session June 6, 1955. The first meeting was held in a combination dining hall and gymnasium. All of the facilities were not complete, and the staff and campers had to spend the first few nights at Ridgecrest. They also walked back and forth to the assembly for meals.

The camp was set up after the model Pickering had established at Camp Ridgecrest for Boys with two five-week sessions. Fifty girls attended the first session and 92 participated in the second session. Susan Harrell, daughter of Mr. and Mrs. W. A. Harrell, was the first camper to enroll. Her father was on the planning committee and was director of the Church Architecture Department of the Baptist Sunday School Board. Her mother served as the first camp hostess.

The spirit of the camp is reflected in its purpose statement in the camp catalogs of the early years:

> Our purpose at Crestridge while we work, play, camp out, live together, is to give the camper opportunity to "lift [her] eyes unto the hill." It is our hope that as she does, she will turn away with a new understanding of "The earth is the Lord's, and the fullness thereof; the world, and they that dwell therein." Applying this understanding to her own life, we hope that she will be able to say positively and proudly, "The Lord is the strength of my life; of whom shall I be afraid?" It is our desire that your daughter advance in truth, courage, growth, perseverance, and purity while at camp. The director and the staff dedicate themselves to give to each camper guidance toward this purpose.

One charter staffer enlisted by Miss Bell for the first session has been on the camp staff every summer. Miss Johnnie Armstrong was land sports director in 1955, program director in 1956, and was named assistant camp director in 1957. When Miss Bell resigned in 1979 to become principal of a Christian school in Florida, Miss Armstrong was named summer director. Armstrong is athletic director at Blue Mountain College, Blue Mountain, Mississippi, and summer director of Camp Crestridge for Girls.

Camp Crestridge for Girls continues to challenge campers to grow in their social, mental, physical, and spiritual life by teaching skills, having Bible study and prayer times, and multiple other activities. The camp song expresses the spirit behind Camp Crestridge for Girls.

The mountains use and point our thoughts to high ideals,
The council fire burns bright to forge the seal;
Our visions and desires are wrought through hearts that kneel,
We pledge our love and loyalty to Camp Crestridge.

The Camps United

In the fall of 1979, Rick Johnson was named director of camps for the Ridgecrest Baptist Conference Center. As coordinator of both camps, he could better serve parents, churches, and others who had children attending both camps. He named Johnnie Armstrong as summer director for Camp Crestridge and Bob Strunk as summer director for Camp Ridgecrest. Strunk is on the faculty of the Athletic Department of Clemson University, Clemson, South Carolina.

The 1981 season was the best overall season in the history of the two camps. Each camp has seen exceptional growth under Johnson's leadership. Both camps stand as monuments to all who have served in their history. The Crestridge motto speaks for all who have a part in the work of the camps: "With my feet on the ground and my heart attuned, I will reach for the stars."

Appendix 3
Ridgecrest Employees: People of Faith

For God is not unrighteous to forget your work and labour of love, which ye have shewed toward his name, in that ye have ministered to the saints, and do minister (Heb. 6:10).

No war was ever won by the generals. Only valiant efforts of the troops assure victories. The conference center employees have faithfully filled the role of "troops" for 90 years. The names of all persons who through the years have given themselves to help Ridgecrest grow cannot be recorded.

Many of today's employees have served for over 15 years; some have served for more than 30 years. Others have retired after similar numbers of years of dedicated service. Every building, every changed life, every life dedicated to the Lord's service stands before God as a tribute to Ridgecrest employees' work.

All the managers who have served at Ridgecrest would readily testify that no institution could have been blessed with better employees. Their faithfulness and sacrificial devotion have carried the conference center many times when a lesser effort would have failed. God has not failed to note one minute of their service, and may we not forget their contribution to His mountain. Their faith helped make Ridgecrest a "mountain of faith."

Perhaps one group, the summer staffers, should have special mention since their service historically has been on a volunteer or semi-volunteer basis. The beginning date of the summer staffer program is not listed in the records of Ridgecrest. However, from the conference center's early days, these staffers have made a unique contribution to the assembly.

About 1955, Loulie Latimer Owens wrote a testimony in *The Ridgecrest Story*, published by Broadman Press. She recalled that the staffer program began during her first visit to Ridgecrest in August 1919. As she looked from her hotel window one morning, she saw some of the regular employees leave guests' "bag and baggage." Within a few hours, students from Mars Hill College arrived to begin serving the guests. According to Mrs. Owens, "that spoiled us, and we've had students ever since."

The staffer salary consisted of room, board, and a very small cash allowance. By the late 60s, that allowance had grown to a starting salary of $5.00 per week. Staffers paid their own travel expenses to and from the assembly.

Summer after summer, these volunteers have chosen Ridgecrest as their place of service. Their choice obviously was not based on money. Neither was it based on prestige or honor. They have performed the most menial tasks with the same care and concern as those who have served on the faculty.

Historically, summer staff workers have been college-age young people. Many staffers returned for several summers until they graduated and accepted employment in their chosen fields. The college-age staffers are supplemented by school teachers and retirees, who serve as hostesses for the hotels.

In the early 70s, the older adult program was greatly expanded to include retired couples and more older singles. This group has proven to be a most enriching part of the conference center. Approximately 40 senior adults serve each summer.

With the increased winter program, Ridgecrest has been able to employ many more year-round employees. Former staffers have filled many of these year-round positions and continue to serve and to strengthen the conference center. Three of the management positions at Ridgecrest currently are filled by former staffers.

Appendix 4
Glorieta Baptist Conference Center

The contribution of Ridgecrest to the lives of Southern Baptists and their churches generated a demand for an additional center to serve the western states of the Convention. A motion was made at the 1938 Southern Baptist Convention to form a committee to study the feasibility of a southwestern assembly. The committee recommended to the 1940 Convention that the matter be dropped.

As the years passed, the need increased. The matter again came before the 1946 Convention, and another committee was appointed. After years of debate, the 1949 Convention, meeting in Oklahoma City, voted to locate a new assembly at Glorieta, New Mexico.[1]

New Mexico Baptists had purchased the 800-acre Breese Ranch at Glorieta in 1948. They offered the property free of charge to Southern Baptists so they could locate the assembly at the ranch. The committee, after accepting the offer, purchased an additional 500 acres adjacent to the Breese site.

Later an additional 1,200 acres were purchased to form the current 2,500-acre campus. Except for the village of Glorieta, the conference center is surrounded by the 380,000-acre Santa Fe National Forest.

Many similarities exist between the Ridgecrest and Glorieta conference centers. Glorieta also is a mountain retreat, located in the majestic Sangre de Cristo mountains. This conference center in the middle of a wilderness is available to accommodate the host of Southern Baptists attending the assembly each year.

The Ridgecrest spiritual and educational emphasis is a vital part of Glorieta. The people and program are first. Manager Larry Haslam expressed it well: "Our primary mission here is to foster education. . . . We're trying to reach people."

The great similarity between the conference centers is God's hand working to carve a Christian ministry in His chosen locations.

Dr. E. A. Herron, the first manager of Glorieta, recognized God's planning. Herron said, "God had the Glorieta ground ready all along."

The years from 1950 to 1952 were years of preparation. Construction of the first unit of New Mexico Hall was started in 1952. Pioneer Week was celebrated at Glorieta in August 1952 with 1,417 persons registered from 18 states.

Three managers have served Glorieta. Dr. E. A. Herron was the first, and served until his retirement in 1966. Mark Short, Jr. served from 1966 to 1973. He resigned to return to the local church ministry. Larry Haslam became manager in 1973 after serving as operations supervisor for Ridgecrest.

And so Glorieta stands today in all of its majesty and splendor, a testimony to all who pass by that Baptists are a vital force, willing to provide in a splendid way for the training and spiritual growth of their people.[2]

---

[1] For a brief history of the early beginning of Glorieta, see Bonnie Ball O'Brien, *Harry P. Stagg: Christian Statesman* (Nashville: Broadman Press, 1976), chap. 8.

[2] *Harry P. Stagg*, 146.

Postscript

Beautiful, spacious, modern Ridgecrest Baptist Conference Center rests in the foothills of the Blue Ridge Mountains, 17 miles east of Asheville, North Carolina. The establishment and growth of this world-class conference center is a tribute to the faith, determination, and sacrifice of its builders. For 90 years, this spiritual retreat and training center has stood as a monument to the glory of God.

Winston Churchill's famous World War II declaration that England's deliverance would require "blood, sweat, and tears" aptly describes the cost of the growth and development of Ridgecrest Baptist Conference Center.

From Ridgecrest's beginning, money, materials, and manpower have been devoted to the center's steady enlargement and modernization. Hundreds of these changes have been chronicled in this book.

Ridgecrest Baptist Conference Center offers a variety of accommodations such as, hotel and motel rooms, dormitories, apartments, and cottages. The center's 714 rooms can accommodate up to 2,500 guests. Ridgecrest also offers a campground with tent and RV sites. Meals are served buffet style. Bernie's Cafe serves pizza, ice cream, and other snacks. The ever-popular Nibble Nook serves a large variety of delicious ice cream and frozen yogurt throughout the summer months. The "mountain of faith" also offers 82 conference rooms and three auditoriums that seat from 400 to 2,600 persons.

Recreational facilities on conference center grounds include tennis, volleyball, softball, and basketball. Four nature and hiking trails through the grounds allow guests to exercise while enjoying the scenery. White water rafting, the beautiful Biltmore Estate, the Blue Ridge Parkway, lofty Mount Mitchell, and many other superb nature scenes are within a few minutes driving time of the conference center. During the winter months, western North Carolina offers numerous ski slopes that are within a one to one-and-a-half hours drive from Ridgecrest.

Recent improvements of the center include the newly remodeled Pritchell Hall lobby, which enables guests to move more swiftly and comfortably through registration and check-out processes. A new addition to the dining hall has shortened the wait time for meals and allows guest to spend this short wait in air-conditioned comfort. Of course, building maintenance and beautification of the center's grounds are ongoing. A new roof recently has been put on Pritchell Hall, and new signs have been placed throughout the campus.

Ridgecrest's mission statement declares:

"Ridgecrest Baptist Conference Center exists to provide life-changing spiritual experiences that nurture vibrant faith, develop effective leaders, encourage healthy families, and mobilize believers for mission and ministry. Ridgecrest will be the first choice for providing spiritual experiences in a Christian atmosphere."

Ridgecrest is open to non-Baptist groups who meet the criteria of the center's mission statement. The conference center is totally self-supporting. It receives no Cooperative Program mission funds.

Ridgecrest is poised for a quantum leap forward. The center's rich history and priceless contribution to the kingdom of God serve as the stimulus for the exciting and challenging Sunday School Board sponsored Capital Campaign Fund program named "Renewing the Place of Renewal." This campaign is designed to modernize both Ridgecrest and Glorieta Baptist conference centers and to position them to meet the ever-changing needs of Christians and churches in the 21st century.